NEW REVISED GUIDE

To The Recommended

COUNTRY INNS

Of New England

Suzy Chapin and Elizabeth Squier

The
Pequot
Press

Chester, Connecticut 06412

HOW THIS GUIDE IS ARRANGED ... The inns
are listed by states and alphabetically by towns within
each state. The states are arranged by a peculiar whim
of the publisher in the following order: Connecticut,
Rhode Island, Massachusetts, Vermont, New Hampshire, and Maine. Starting on page *222* is a special
index arranged by areas to help you in planning a trip.

YOU WILL FIND some pointing fingers 🖝 🖝 🖝 🖝 🖝
scattered about the write-ups. While we have not rated the
inns, when we found something particularly outstanding or
different, we inserted a 🖝 as a special plaudit. And at the
end of some of the write-ups, you might find these symbols:

$\mathcal{E}$ – stands for Elizabeth

$\mathcal{S}$ – stands for Suzy

This was to give us the opportunity to add an individual note
on a special, personal delight.

Library of Congress Catalog Card Number 73–83255
ISBN–0–87106–070–1
Manufactured in the United States of America
THIRD EDITION

How To Enjoy This Guide

WHEN we first started writing THE GUIDE TO THE RECOMMENDED COUNTRY INNS OF NEW ENGLAND several years ago, we had no idea that there were so many folks who were tired of the monotony of motels and thruway hotels, and were willing to exchange certain conveniences for the infinitely more warming pleasures of a country inn.

ENTHUSIASM from innkeepers, inn guests, armchair travellers, and memories of our last jaunt, have again sent us inncreeping in order to update and increase our GUIDE. In this edition you will find that 17 new inns have been added.

ALTHOUGH we have made every attempt to be up-to-date, please realize that prices and menus are subject to change, as are innkeepers. If you are planning to stay overnight, or even a very special dinner out, we recommend that you call ahead so that you will not be disappointed. Many of the inns are small, and it would be a shame to travel a long distance and not get in. *And* we can not always prescribe an inn's temperament. Just as seasons change, so does man. By our descriptions and comments, we have tried to indicate whether an inn would be appropriate for children, pets, young couples, elderly folk. If you are planning a weeks' stay, you might send for the inn's literature to help you decide. But don't forget, the very reason you are passing up motel or hotel is for the bit of adventure and surprise you will find sitting in a weathered farmhouse, eating country cooking, chatting with a discovered friend, finding new delight in a very old tradition.

DON'T become distressed because an inn you like may not be listed. Please understand that our definition of a country inn is that it *must* have lodging, as well as good food, and *must* be open essentially year round. It is, however, all right if they close for a month or a bit more for refurbishing, or, as an instance, to avoid the uniquely New England "mud season" of late winter. If you have an inn recommendation, please write us so that we can include it in our next edition. So enjoy . . . This GUIDE was compiled for you, fellow lovers of the New England country inn.

Suzy & Elizabeth

Old Farms Inn
Avon, Connecticut
06001

Innkeepers: Belle Young and Al Ginewsky
Telephone: 203-677-2818
Rooms: 5, all with bath, air conditioned.
Rates: Single $17, double $21.
Facilities: Open all year. Restaurant closed Monday. Lunch and Dinner. Bar. Parking. Swimming. Restaurant accessible to wheelchair. Also there is an adjacent motel.

HOW TO GET THERE:

15 minutes west of Hartford at the intersection of Routes 44 and 10.

There have been people living here at this crossroads for over 300 years, and though Old Farms has been an Inn, as such, for only about fifty of them, there is history galore in this collection of buildings, old and new. The Forge Room was originally a blacksmith's shop, and many of the antique tools are on display there. The guest rooms are few and often in use by members of the Inn family, so be sure to make a reservation. Though the word "motel" is an anathema to us and our publisher, there is, across the street from this Inn a most comfortable place to stay, and when our wheelchair person is traveling with us, we stay there.

The food at Old Farms Inn is good, served by pleasant people who do not rush you, even on a hectic Saturday evening. There is a large wine list, and 🖛 you can begin Sunday brunch at 11:00 a.m. This Inn is located at a busy crossroads and is a wonderful meeting or resting place for gals like us who love to shop.

E: Book me in for a week so I can visit all the fabulous shops in the area at my leisure.

S: It is so wonderful to have a place like this to flee to when I am school-hopping.

> *Our sympathy for the hardships of our forebears should be somewhat mitigated by the fact that they had the best of country inns.*

Griswold Inn
Essex, Connecticut
06426

Innkeepers: William G. Winterer, A. W. Lovell
Telephone: 203-767-1812
Rooms: 20 rooms, some with private baths.
Rates: EP, $18 to $26 daily, depending upon occupancy and
facilities. Twin and double beds both available. All
air conditioned.
Facilities: Open every day but Christmas. Complimentary
Continental Breakfast served to house guests. Lunch
and Dinner. Famous Hunt Breakfast on Sundays.
Bar. Parking.

HOW TO GET THERE:
Connecticut Turnpike Exit 69, to Conn. 9, the Inn is ½
mile east of Exit 3. Daily rail service from New York
and Boston.

Essex is a special place, and the "Gris" is one of the things that makes this river town so appealing. Essex is a town that was settled long before the Revolution, that is still a living, breathing, working place, not a recreated museum of a town.

When you come in from the cold to the welcome of the pot-bellied stove, or draw up to one of the crackling fireplaces you are doing what others have for two hundred years before you. Now in summer, there is air-conditioned comfort in the great old bar. You can lunch in the cool dimness of the Library, or the Gun Room. The collection of Currier and Ives prints at the Inn is worthy of a museum. Dine in the Steamboat Room, where the mural on the far wall floats gently, making you feel that you are really on the River. Old-time banjo music Friday and Sunday nights, sea chanteys Monday nights, add to the fun.

In summer, sailors from the far corners of the earth make Essex a port of call, others come in by car, or arrive in Old Saybrook by Amtrak. However the people come, they know there is a welcome at the friendly old inn on Main street, just a short walk from the harbor.

You can buy a yacht to carry you round the world in Essex, or a pair of Topsiders to keep your footing in your Boston Whaler.

E: My favorite thing about the Gris? It has to be the antique popcorn machine in the bar.

S: They have a new expresso machine which makes divine coffee.

Copper Beech Inn
Ivoryton, Town of Essex
Connecticut
06442

Innkeepers: Robert and Jo McKenzie
Telephone: 203-767-0330
Rooms: 5, Double or twin with private bath.
Rates: $22–$25.
Facilities: Open all year. Closed on Mondays. Lunch and
Dinner served. Bar. Parking. Bedboards. Greenhouse
open Tuesday thru Sunday 4:30 to closing.

HOW TO GET THERE:
Located 1 mile west of Conn. Route 9, exit 3 or 4.
Follow signs to Ivoryton.

There is a magnificent copper beech that shades the front lawn of the Copper Beech Inn. This grand old Inn had fallen into rack and ruin, but Jo and Bob McKenzie had the vision to see, a wonderfully restored country Inn.

The dining rooms, there are three of them, all have comfortable Chippendale Queen Anne chairs with good sized tables, spread widely apart for gracious dining. Fresh flowers are everywhere, and the waiters serving ☛ the excellent fare are friendly and efficient. The chef, Raymond Terrill, is a prize winner, and the food bears witness to this.

The rooms in the Inn are color coordinated, comfortable and large. The baths are a great combination of old and new and a wonder to see. ☛ There is a new cocktail lounge made from an old greenhouse, located behind the Inn. All you do is look up to see the stars, moon, rain or snow. What a way to relax. Unusual plants hang all over the greenhouse, soft lounge chairs done in a pretty floral pattern, with the right sized cocktail tables with shell laden hurricane lamps lit on each one. ☛ The bar has six very comfortable chairs, and a smiling bartender named Hank, who has the most unusual sideburns.

Reservations are a must, to stay, or just to dine. It's worth the trip no matter how far you must travel.

$\mathcal{E}$: The rooms are utterly charming, with antiques and unbelievable old bathrooms.☛ The little dining porch with its white wicker furniture and crisp green hanging baskets is the place for a rendezvous luncheon.

$\mathcal{S}$: A sprig of watercress beside the paté, the stemmed crystal glasses holding the rabbits' ear folded napkins, the careful attention to every detail by the delightful owners, the darling McKenzie daughters, there's not a thing I just don't adore about this Inn.

The Homestead Inn
Belle Haven, Greenwich, Connecticut
06830

Innkeepers: Cal Estes, Vincent Morino
Telephone: 203-869-7500
Rooms: 25, all with bath.
Rates: Twin beds,$28–$30;double bed,$22–$24;singles, $20–
$24; suites, $34–$38.
Facilities: The Inn is open all year. The Dining Room is
closed on Sunday. Breakfast 7 days for house guests.
No lunch on Saturday or Sunday. Dinner 6 nights.
Bar. Ample parking. Swimming pool. Memorial Day
to Labor Day, Bar and Bar-B-Que at poolside every
day except Monday.

HOW TO GET THERE:

Take Exit 3 off Connecticut Turnpike (I-95). At Exit,
turn toward Railroad Bridge. At Bridge, turn left, go
two blocks to a dead end. Turn left again and go up hill
¼ mile to Homestead sign on right. The easy way is
to take the train from Grand Central to Greenwich
Station. A 3 minute taxi trip to the Inn.

Over the electric organ in the bar there is a lovely needlepoint sign: "Accomplished Musicians are Invited to Play." And I am sure they do, in among the fish tanks, in this old Inn, high on a hill above the turmoil of the town. Gracious living and dining have been taking place within these walls since 1799. For all that, the place has a Victorian air. Perhaps it is the ➤vast porches that sweep around the house on two sides, a perfect spot for summer lunching or dining. This is a popular watering spot, so be sure to reserve. ➤ There is a very interesting buffet at lunch time, not ordinary things to eat. Also the omlets, English style, very brown and puffy, are good.

The pool is delightful in summer, and there have been many guests who return, year in and year out, to make the Homestead Inn their summer place.

ℰ: Downtown in Greenwich there is a bakery that makes something called Sarah Bernhardts. Immorally good.

𝒮: When you sit on the porch you feel as if you are a bird, you are right *in* the tree tops.

> *To eat merely to live is a crime against man for which the gibbet is inadequate punishment.*

Meetinghouse Inn
Litchfield, Connecticut
06759

Innkeepers: Raymond Sass, Jeff Guerette
Telephone: 203-567-8744
Rooms: 6, each with bath; one large suite.
Rates: Suite $50, double $30, single $25.
Facilities: Open all year. Full Breakfast for house guests. Luncheon and Dinner. Bar. Ample parking. Wheelchair ramp for restaurant only. 15 minutes to Mohawk Mountain skiing. Swimming, boating and fishing in Bantam Lake, 3 miles away.

HOW TO GET THERE:

Bus from New York will let you off in front of the Inn. 94 miles from New York, 134 miles from Boston, 35 miles from Hartford. From I-84 in Danbury take Route 7 north to Route 202 to Litchfield. From Waterbury take Route 8 to Route 118, then west on Route 202. The Inn is just west of the Litchfield Green on Route 202.

Raymond and Pamela Sass and Jeff Guerette have taken a tumbledown inn that was moldering quietly on a hillside in Litchfield, painted the outside a warm golden color, completely redecorated the inside and returned this colonial inn to its former glory. Their new sign promises sustenance, libation and accommodation, which is but the bare bones of the story. The public rooms are comfortably arranged, the more formal Continental Room on the right, the Bar and the Plant Room on the left, as you come into the spacious center hall. The Plant Room is festooned with two dozen hanging baskets. In summer there is a spacious terrace for outdoor dining. The waitresses wear gingham skirts, everyone moves at a smart pace and the service is happy.

The food is not fancy, but it is very good. Every night there is something special, and Saturday and Sunday noons the Champagne Brunch fills the house. The Inn serves the best Eggs Benedict in the Litchfield Hills. Salads are crisp and inviting, served in large wooden bowls. Drinks come in Out-size glasses and are delicious. We hope there is some Amaretto Creme Parfait left for your dessert; it is an experience.

Enthusiastic about this place? You *know* it's true. The bedrooms (only a few, so reserve ahead) have been beautifully restored with the help of a local decorator. Sort of colonial, but with a very with-it touch of here and now.

Ɛ: Happy days in the merry bar carry me back to Litchfield.

S: Tuck me up in the room with the patchwork walls. Let me stroll barefoot on that scarlet carpet.

The Roger Sherman Inn
New Canaan, Connecticut
06840

Innkeepers: Walter Maliszewski and Steve Zur
Telephone: 203-966-4541
Rooms: 10 rooms, all with bath, all air conditioned
Rates: $12–$30
Facilities: Open all year. Closed on Sunday. Breakfast for
house guests only. Lunch and Dinner. Bar. Television
in most guest rooms. Ample Parking.

HOW TO GET THERE:
Exit 37 from Merritt Parkway will take you directly
to Inn. Or take Main Street out of New Canaan to
Oenoke Road. The Inn is on the right.

Built in 1740, once the home of Roger Sherman, one of the Signers of the Declaration of Independence, this friendly Inn still offers a warm welcome to the tired traveler. The cuisine may be a bit more continental than it was in the early days, but we are all a bit more sophisticated today. There is music in the dining room here on the weekend. If you are so inclined there is a wonderful Nature Center just across the street from the Inn, and the summer theater at Westport is still a popular place to go on a warm evening.

The guest rooms are large and comfortable. There are even two and three room apartments so you can bring the whole family. In the summer there is "Veranda Dining." In winter, lead me to the "Publick Tap Room."

New Canaan is a lovely little town with some very attractive shops, among them one of the very best bakeries we have ever run across. There is a good book shop, some fine dress shops, and antique shops. Also a place called "Fat Tuesday," reputed to be the mecca of all the local swingers. Rumor only.

If you want a nice place to hole up for a week, or a month, give The Roger Sherman a try. The food is good, and the surroundings delightful.

Man has tendencies of many temperatures, the warmest of which is hospitality.

Mountain View Inn
Norfolk, Connecticut
06058

Innkeepers: Karl and Joan Jokinen, Proprietors: Helen and George Linonis
Telephone: 203-542-5595
Rooms: 7 rooms, 11 baths.
Rates: In winter, $14.50 single, $19.50 double. A dollar more per person in summer.
Facilities: Open all year. Breakfast, Lunch and Dinner served. Bar. Restaurant accessible to wheelchair.

HOW TO GET THERE:

Take Route 44 east from Route 7. The Inn is located on Route 272 in Norfolk.

Norfolk seems like a town that time forgot. The Mountain View Inn is a rambling old white house, clinging to a hillside just a short stroll from the center of this charming little town. There is a very active Curling Club in town, one of the more obscure winter sports. The house was built around 1850. There is a maple-shaded veranda where summertime dining is a pleasure. If you are a winter guest you will be welcomed with blazing fireplaces.

The young folks are doing the work, with a helping hand from the older ones. The chef is as handy with a paintbrush as he is with a pastry brush. He can paper walls, too. It is well to be versatile when you run a country inn. There's a country store here, it moves around according to the weather, but if you look, you can find it.

If you want to get away from it all, without driving all day, take a trip up to Norfolk. If music is your forte, the Yale Music School is right here in Norfolk, with concerts in the Music Shed all summer long.

&: The tables made from old sewing machines are just charming.

S: There is an informality to this place that appeals to me. Camaraderie between the guests and the hosts relaxes me.

> *If I ever find an inn that bakes fresh macaroons daily, I shall rent a room for a hundred years.*

Silvermine Tavern
Norwalk, Connecticut
06850

Innkeeper: Francis C. Whitman, Jr.
Telephone: 203-847-4558
Rooms: 10 all with bath.
Rates: Single, $16–$18; Double-bed Room, $27–$30; Twin-bed Room, $27–$28–$30.
Facilities: Inn open all year except closed Tuesday—October to May. Breakfast for house guests only, Luncheon and Dinner. Bar. Television in parlor. 6 fireplaces in public rooms.

HOW TO GET THERE:

From New York, take Exit 38 from the Merritt Parkway. Turn left onto Route 123. Turn left at the Fire House onto Silvermine Avenue which will take you directly to the Inn. From I-95 take Exit 15 onto Rt 7. Take Exit 2. Turn right onto New Canaan Ave. First right onto Rt 123. First right by Firehouse onto Silvermine Ave.

Close to everything, when you are at the Silvermine Tavern you are a world away in time. If you wish, you can stroll by the waterfall and feed the ducks and swans on the Millpond. The colonial crossroads village known as Silvermine has been swallowed up by the surrounding towns of Norwalk, Wilton and New Canaan, but the Tavern still lies at the heart of a suburban community of great beauty. It is one of the most popular dining places in the area, known for the delicious New England traditional food. Thursday night is set aside for a fantastic Buffet Supper, featuring steaks, fried chicken, many salads, and everything to go with it. Sunday Buffet Brunch features twenty different choices.

Silvermine Tavern is furnished with old Oriental rugs, antiques, old portraits, comfortable chairs and sofas near the huge fireplaces. The dining room which overlooks the river, is decorated with over a thousand antiques, primarily old farm tools and household artifacts. In summer there is a brick-floored patio for al fresco dining. The guest rooms are comfortably furnished, many of them with old-fashioned tester beds.

Across the road you will find an authentic Country Store. In the back room there is a museum of antique tools and gadgets and a fine collection of Currier & Ives prints. Drive along the little back roads that lead to the Tavern. The Silvermine Guild of Artists is well-known, and you are not too far from Stratford or Westport if the theater is your thing. Be sure to reserve ahead because Silvermine is very popular.

We sat together round a single table and talked and heard each other in the quiet of the inn.

Bee and Thistle Inn
Old Lyme, Connecticut
06371

Innkeepers: Gene and Barbara Bellows
Telephone: 203-434-7861
Rooms: 8, 6 with bath, 2 share. Double or twin beds.
Rates: $20–$29.
Facilities: Open all year. Breakfast, Lunch and Dinner. Brunch on Sundays. Dinner reservations 24 hours in advance except for house guests. No Bar. BYO. Private parties. Bicycles for guests.

HOW TO GET THERE:

Traveling north on Route 95, take Exit 70. At bottom of ramp turn left and first right to traffic light. Turn left. The Inn is on the left past the Old Lyme Art Association. Traveling south on Route 95, take Exit 70. Turn right at the bottom of the ramp, and the Inn is on the left.

If you are looking for a country inn that is like a lovely country house, seek no further. The Bee and Thistle, set among wide lawns, beneath tall trees, provides abundance of comfort. Breakfast in bed, on a flower bedecked tray. The softest supercale sheets and eyelet trimmed blanket covers adorn the beds. From the back of the house, you can see the Lieutenant River meandering through the meadows toward the Sound.

There is no bar, but you can bring your own supplies; set-ups are available. The menu is limited to one or two entrees, several fresh vegetables are served along with homemade soups. Reservations are a must at least one day in advance. Dinners are served by candlelight and the dining rooms are filled with flowers. Frequently the sounds of Barbara and other musicians waft through the dining rooms. Early ballads with dulcimer and guitar or baroque sonatas played with recorders. Plants, books, and magazines are in the lounge near the fireplace. There are 6 fireplaces in this old house built in 1796 as a private residence.

The Old Lyme Art Association is nearby, close enough for a stroll. And there are many things to do in the area. The summer theatre at Ivoryton, Goodspeed Opera House in East Haddam, and the charming river town of Essex is nearby.

$\mathcal{E}$: The Sunday brunch is yummy.

$\mathcal{S}$: Breakfast in bed beckons me.

> *The good morning greeting and the good night good wish can only be found in a country inn.*

Old Lyme Inn
Old Lyme, Connecticut
06371

Innkeepers: Kenneth and Diana Milne
Telephone: 203-434-2600
Rooms: 5, all with bath, plus a sixth room for the handicapped.
Rates: $30 double.
Facilities: Open all year. Mondays the restaurant only is closed. Continental Breakfast served with rooms. Lunch and Dinner.

HOW TO GET THERE:

Traveling north on Route 95 take Exit 70, immediately on the west side of the bridge. At bottom of ramp turn left. Take first right to traffic light and turn left. Inn is on the right. Traveling south on Route 95 take Exit 70. At bottom of ramp turn right. Inn is on the right.

When traveling on Route 95 north or south, you are just a few minutes away from this lovely restored Inn.

As you enter the door, to your left is a large cocktail lounge with comfortable chairs and a bar that seats 6. The back bar, found in Philadelphia, is about 100 years old and is worth the trip alone to see it. Of course while you are there, and if it is after 4 o'clock, they have a special menu for the late afternoon and early evening nibblers, like smoked salmon, patés and more.

The young chef Steve Wilkinson, spent 3 years in San Francisco before coming to Old Lyme and is an artist at butter sculpture. The pastry shells are all homemade and so tender. Steve also does things with desserts that should be illegal they are so good. A real plus for the Inn is all of the fresh soup stock and wait 'til you taste the soup. One of the nights I had Filet Mignon with green peppercorn sauce. Others in the party had Grilled Sea Bass, Quinelle of Halibut, and Chicken served in cider with apples. The artichokes have a lemon mayonnaise sauce that is very different. Also all vegetables are fresh.

The chairs are blue velvet throughout the Inn, and very comfortable. The rooms have new beds and are decorated in fine taste.

Sassy is the Inn cat who will greet you at the door.

&: The bar is a real favorite spot of mine, with a bartender who remembers what you drink.

S: The private dining room for 8 to 12 people is a nice way to entertain.

The Elms
Ridgefield, Connecticut
06877

Innkeepers: Mario Scala and Robert Scala
Telephone: 203-438-2541
Rooms: 14, 12 with bath.
Rates: Single, $15.00; double, $20.00.
Facilities: Closed on Christmas Day and Wednesday. Breakfast for house guests only. Luncheon and Dinner. Bar. Ample Parking. Fireplaces in every room.

HOW TO GET THERE:

The Inn is located at 500 Main Street, Ridgefield. The bus from New York will drop you at the door. You can also get a train to Ridgefield. If you come by car, Ridgefield lies about 3 miles off Route 7. Turn left at Branchville on Route 102, or if you are coming down 7 from Danbury take Route 35, which turns off to the right.

It is truly delightful to find a marvelous Continental restaurant in an authentic country Inn that dates back about two centuries. The house was built in 1760 and became an Inn in 1799, and has been one ever since. This charming old house, with huge fireplaces and beamed ceilings is one of the best places to eat in New England. The Scala brothers have a beautiful menu, and the food is exceptional. Friendly waiters wish you "Good appetite" as they present hot plates full of excellent things to eat. Do try Veal Venus—a veal cutlet sauteed, then covered with purée of mushroom and hollandaise sauce glace. The deep dish apple pie that concludes the meal is subtly seasoned, tart not too sweet, melting in the mouth. Plan to stay awhile, this place is too good to rush away.

There is a comfortable four poster in one of the quiet rooms upstairs, or perhaps you would prefer the one with the maple spool twin beds. There are concerts in the park in summer. And a lovely clutch of shops within strolling distance.

&: Any place that serves A Coupe Elizabeth for dessert gets my nod. Would you believe Bing cherries bathed in Cherry Herring, sprinkled with cinnamon, poured over vanilla ice cream? It is only too true.

> *Where else, in all good conscience, could I stay but at a country inn.*

Stonehenge
Ridgefield, Connecticut
06877

Innkeepers: David Davis and Douglas Seville
Telephone: 203-438-6511
Rooms: 8, all with private bath and television.
Rates: $30.00–$40.00.
Facilities: Open all year except Good Friday, Election Day
and closed Tuesday. Breakfast, Lunch and Dinner.
Bar. Parking. Superb food and service.

HOW TO GET THERE:
Route 7, Ridgefield. The sign, coming south from Route
84, is not very large, on the left.

"You can't go home again" said Thomas Wolfe, but you can go back to Stonehenge. Under the direction of two gentlemen, David Davis and Douglas Seville, this beautiful country Inn is blooming again. The chef, ➤Ans Benderer, Swiss born and trained, is nonpareil. The setting is still serenely beautiful, with the old white farmhouse overlooking the lake, swan bedecked, with Canadian geese and ducks stopping in on their migratory journeys. The service, under the skilled direction of Maitre d'Hotel, Gieri Albin, is what we always dreamed it should be, deft, quiet, pleasant, knowledgeable.

For a quiet dinner a deux, reserve a table in the bar. Address yourself seriously to the food. The appetizers are unusual, not to be skipped over lightly.   The soups are poetic.   The trout is live. "How long ago?" asked Suzy's husband. "About five minutes," was the reply, "the time it takes to come from the 'trout house.' " If you are tired of the "same old thing" book yourself into Stonehenge for a long weekend and find out what "haut cuisine" is all about. It is expensive, but worth every centime.

The main dining room, with wide windows overlooking the lake, is panelled, and glowed with warmth on the rainiest spring day. The mallards were amusing to watch while we enjoyed our lunch. The chef will not disclose the secret of his salad dressing, he keeps changing it. Whatever he does, it is perfect.

Many of the things we loved so much are still served at Stonehenge. The inventive touch with vegetables, the care taken with the sauces, all reflect the dedication with which M. Benderer approaches his task.

E: Our favorite room is the big one in the front of the main house. Any season, any weather, it is a home away for us.

S: Cheers for the Innkeeper who when asked, "Breakfast for house guests only, I assume?" answered instantly, "We will serve breakfast to anyone who comes in, a little informal, perhaps, but we're always glad to see them."

Old Riverton Inn
Riverton, Connecticut
06065

Innkeepers: Mr. and Mrs. James Zucco
Telephone: 203-379-8678
Rooms: 10, all with bath.
Rates: $8.50 per person and up, all year, complimentary breakfast.
Facilities: Open all year, closed Monday, Tuesday and Christmas. Dining room closed January & February. Breakfast for house guests and ◣ fishermen. Lunch and Dinner. Bar. Parking. Dining room accessible to wheelchairs.

HOW TO GET THERE:
Route 8 to Winsted, turn right on Route 20.

Gallop in to the Hobby Horse Bar at the Old Riverton Inn, and be served a drink by a charming Filipino
bartender whose nickname is Hoppy. Almost all the help
at this old stagecoach stop has been here, with the Zuccos
since they took over in 1946. The waitresses in their crisp
ruffled aprons move deftly around the low-ceilinged dining
room. The breads and pastries are homemade and better
than anything a modern day grandmother makes. The
Grindstone Terrace, enclosed to make a lovely dining room,
is in use all year round. Riverton is the home of the original Hitchcock Chair Factory, indeed, you sit upon Hitchcock chairs in the dining room.

Upstairs, a world away from the subdued bustle below,
there is a comfortable sitting room, papered in our favorite
Paisley pattern, and ten lovely bedrooms. This is one of
the most modestly priced, attractive and inviting inns we
have found. Mrs. Zucco tells us that most of their guests
return year after year, and word of mouth has been the
only advertising. If you haven't stayed at the Old Riverton
Inn make a reservation today.

E: I would like to sit forever on a hobby horse at the bar,
drinking, what else, martinis.

S: Garden rooms are my favorite spots, and this is one
of the most engaging I've seen in many a long day.

Under Mountain Inn

Under Mountain Inn
Salisbury, Connecticut
06068

Innkeepers: Lou and Doris Schroeter
Telephone: 203-435-0242
Rooms: 7, all with private bath.
Rates: $25.00–$35.00.
Facilities: The Inn is closed for 2 or 3 weeks in March, and also on Monday and Tuesday. Breakfast for house guests, Brunch on Sunday 12:00–3:00, and Dinner Wednesday through Saturday, 5:00–10:00, and Sunday 1:00–9:00.

HOW TO GET THERE:
Take Route 41 North from Salisbury, the Inn is on the left.

What joy to find one of our old inns that had closed up reopened under new ownership; Lou Schroeter used to own The Morgan House in Lee, Massachusetts. Under Mountain Inn is really an old colonial house. The bar was constructed from wide, wide old boards found hidden in the attic. Boards this wide were made from trees known before the Revolution as "King's Wood."

The food, however, is now slightly sophisticated, with such delightful things as Escargots in Mushroom Caps, Steak au Poivre, Poached Salmon, Sweetbreads. 🐟 The soups and breads are homemade. If you have room, try an apple pancake.

Ɛ: Pat Chris, the friendly inn dog, on the head for me.

S: Weather permitting, have a drink of the terrace. That's my place.

The glowing carriage lamp beside the door of a country inn when viewed through a cold rain erases the rigors of the day and promises a fine, fine evening.

White Hart Inn
Salisbury, Connecticut
06068

Innkeeper: John Harney
Telephone: 203-435-2511
Rooms: 25 rooms, 7 of them air conditioned motel types, suitable for wheelchairs, 10 rooms with air conditioning in the Inn, all with private bath and telephone.
Rates: Single, $16–$20, Double, $18.50–$24.50. Single in motel, $18–$24, double in motel, $22–$28, extra bed in room, $3.50.
Facilities: air conditioned dining room and patio, with ramp, screened summer dining porch, Colonial Tap Room. Breakfast, Lunch and Dinner served.

HOW TO GET THERE:

Turn off Route 7 at Canaan, and turn west on Route 44. The White Hart is on the green in the center of Salisbury.

Named for an older White Hart Inn in Salisbury, England, the American cousin has been taking care of wayfaring strangers since 1867. Restored by the Ford family (Hotchkiss School alumni) there are 15 rooms in the inn, plus 7 air conditioned motel rooms adjoining the main building. John Harney has been running the inn for the past sixteen years, and has it well in hand. ☞ There is a fascinating lady named Olive Dubois who makes a whole gingerbread village each year at Christmas, as well as keeping order in the sometimes hectic life of the innkeeper.

There is a country store spilling over into the lobby, with good home baked goods, health foods, and Mr. Harney's own brand of tea.

☞ The spacious dining room, tap room and patio terrace give ample room for dining. The food is sound American fare, served in an atmosphere of Old New England. The rooms are those typical of a country inn, there are a couple of suites.

E: Compulsive shopper that I am, I was more than contented with the country store.

S: Directly across the street from the Inn I found the Housatonic Book Shop, necessary to my peace of mind, as I am a compulsive reader.

> *Man's cruelty to man knows almost no horizons. His continued existence, however, is justified when he says to a stranger, "Come in."*

Sweet Meadows Inn
Narragansett, Rhode Island
02882

Innkeepers: Mr. and Mrs. McLaughlin

Telephone: 401-783-7315

Rooms: Inn: 3 Double Rooms, 1 Single Room; Motel: 5 Double Units.

Rates: Summer: Inn: $30.00 per day Double, $15.00 Single; Motel: $29.00 per day.
Winter: Inn and Motel $20.
All units have private baths.

Facilities: Continental Breakfast, Lunch and Dinner. Sunday Buffet Brunch. Closed on Monday. TV in every room. Air-conditioned. Lovely gardens.

HOW TO GET THERE:

On Route 108, off US Route 1, Narragansett, Rhode Island.

How sweet it is at Sweet Meadows Inn! Hidden away
on Route 108, it basks in its beautiful garden, welcoming the
weary, hungry traveller. An enormous St. Bernard named
Holly, might open one eye as you walk up to the door, and
if you are lucky you will see a cat named Gertrude, who really
owns the place.

Mr. McLaughlin is restoring the formal gardens
that were laid out in 1901, and an artist friend has beautifully
repaired and restored the exquisite antique wallpaper in the
main dining room. Behind the Inn itself, there are some
attractive apartments, and everywhere there are trees and
flowers.

There is a fine chef who is justifiably proud of
his "Boneless Roast Duckling." This is one of the specialities
of this House, but must be ordered ahead, so the chef has
time to bone out the duckling. Fresh, fresh seafood is available from the local fishing fleet.

As we walked through the lovely garden we met a
gangling young red setter who seriously destroys all Holly's
serious mein. The charm and warmth of this lovely place
make it a real winner. The Friday night buffet is outstanding, centered on a magnificent roast beef, with many delicious, exotic dishes.

&: The view from the dining room is glorious.

S: The smiling faces that welcome you to this unique Inn
keep us returning.

New Shamrock Cliff Hotel
Newport, Rhode Island
02840

Innkeeper: John Reber, Ass't. Manager: Nelson Thompson
Telephone: 401-847-7777
Rooms: 25, all with bath.
Rates: July 1-Labor Day, $50 single, $75 double. Off season: from $20 single to $40 double.
Facilities: The Inn is closed from January through mid-April. Otherwise open every day. Dining room. Breakfast, Lunch and Dinner served. Television in cocktail lounge. Ample parking. Marina. Entertainment in summer.

HOW TO GET THERE:
From the south, cross Newport Bridge and turn right on Route 238, keep right on Ocean Drive.

This Newport Summer Cottage was built in 1895, and remained a private home until 1956. ☛ The location is superb, overlooking the entrance to Narragansett Bay, with a sweeping view of the Atlantic Ocean. High on a wind-swept hill, a guest at the Shamrock Cliff can see anything that enters the Harbor. If you come by boat you can tie up at the private dock and stroll up to lunch or dine. The main dining room, breakfast room and cocktail lounge are additions to the original house, and unfortunately, not of the same marvelous granite construction. However, when you are safely inside you have eyes only for the magnificent panorama of sky and water that surrounds you.

☛ Our favorite room is up two winding flights of stairs, ending in a vaulted tower room that has a wrap around balcony, surely fit for any Juliet. You feel that you are truly on top of the world.

The food is New York modern, with a good array of steaks and seafood. Calorie watchers are recognized, at least at lunch, and one of the nice touches at dinner is the iced relish bowl.

Let us escape for a day, or better a week, and hide away in a country inn.

Larchwood Inn
Wakefield, Rhode Island
02879

Innkeeper: Francis J. Browning
Telephone: 401-783-5454
Rooms: 11 double, 6 with private bath, 3 others share.
Rates: $9 to $22.
Facilities: Restaurant, bar, formal gardens, Breachway
 Room, for weddings, Buttery, small private parties,
 open all year.

HOW TO GET THERE:

Route 1A, Wakefield, Rhode Island.

Over the fireplace in the homey bar is carved "Fast by an Ingle Bleezing Finely" a quotation from the Scots' Robert Burns. ➤His birthday, January 25th, is celebrated here, and last year a couple of pipers come over from Connecticut to help the party along. The Scotch flavor is all over this homelike country inn. The present innkeeper, Francis J. Browning took over from his in-laws, the Camerons, who had been running things for the past quarter of a century. The Tam O'Shanter Cocktail Lounge serves up a delectable lunch each day except Sunday, and there are four other lovely rooms for dining, or private entertaining.

Come summer there is a patio in the garden where meals are served. The Inn is situated in the heart of Rhode Island's beautiful South County. Salt water beaches for bathing, fishing and sunning are close by. In the winter it is only a short drive to Pine Top and Yawgoo Valley for Skiing.

Rhode Island isn't all that big, you know, so it's never very far from anywhere to the Larchwood Inn.

A good inn, good food, a warm bed and a loving woman . . . heaven can be another time.

The Lord Jeffrey
Amherst, Massachusetts
01002

Innkeeper: Tim Rauton; General Mgr. Edwin Anderson.
Telephone: 413-253-2576
Rooms: 46, air conditioned.
Rates: Single, $10–$15, Double, $22–$25.
Facilities: TV in every room. Tavern, dining rooms, serving
Continental Breakfast, Lunch and Dinner. Open 7
days a week since 1926.

HOW TO GET THERE:

I91, to Route 5 or Route 10, located on The Green, in
the middle of town.

Lord Jeffrey Amherst was a soldier of the king, and for his brave deeds this town was named for him, the college was named for him, and the lovely country inn, carries his name as well. Although the Inn was built in the twenties, it looks as if it has been here for centuries. ➤ There is outdoor dining in the summer in a delightful garden. Winter brings bright fires in the fieldstone fireplaces, with the folk singer raising his voice in the bar.

Amherst is a busy college town, for there are many colleges in Amherst and nearby. ➤ Emily Dickinson dwelt unseen, during her lifetime, but now hundreds of people come to celebrate her birthday.

E: Any inn that serves Eggs Benedict for lunch is HIGH on my list, and when it is served in the beautiful dining room at The Lord Jeff, I am doubly happy.

S: The lovely library room that can be used for private parties caught my eye, but I'm really in love with the wisteria vine in the garden. Oh, that garden!

> *There is no definition of a proper inn. Like night and day it either is or is not.*

High Brewster
Satucket Road, Brewster, Massachusetts
02631

Innkeepers: W. C. Arbuckle and Walter E. Hyde
Telephone: 617-896-3636
Rooms: 1 double room with bath, 2 doubles and 1 single
 share bath.
Rates: MAP $27–$44.
Facilities: Open all year. Dining room closed Sunday, Monday and Tuesday, but private parties can be held on
 those nights. Breakfast for house guests only. No
 lunch. No bar. Bring your own. Set-ups available.
 Pleasant terrace for pre-prandial drinking. Dining
 area accessible for wheelchair. Dinner served 6:30 to
 9:00. *By reservation only.*

HOW TO GET THERE:
 Satucket Road goes to the left off 6-A. Look for an old
 mill on the left, the next property is High Brewster.

High Brewster is such a special place that we must warn you to reserve way ahead of time if you want to go, and you must not be disappointed if they can't take you. It is so small and so charming. You will most likely be greeted when you arrive by a ▰▰bulldog named Sibyl, followed shortly thereafter by one or both of the owners. There are roosters, ceramic, glass, straw, metal, whatever, all over. Even on a dreary winter day the windows are full of flowering plants, and in the summer the garden is lovely.

There are several dining rooms, with a variety of different shaped tables. Private parties are a big thing here, so if you are nearby and want to entertain a group, call early, and we can promise you a party you won't soon forget.

There are lots of lovely antiques, and the house itself is warmly welcoming. ▰▰The menu has things like Oyster Bisque, Clams Marengo or Marinated Beef to begin. There is usually a choice of meat or fish, salad, and a choice of desserts, Lemon Mousse, Mocha Chocolate Pie, and always Mixed Fresh Fruit. You sort of take "potluck", but this is such superior luck, we know you'll enjoy it.

℘: The very steep back stairs that lead right down to the kitchen enchant me. Can you imagine running down in your housecoat to get an early cup of coffee in one of those cookie cutter motels? It's the kind of thing you can do at High Brewster if you're lucky enough to get in.

Inn of the Golden Ox
Brewster, Massachusetts
02631

Innkeepers: Charles and Ruth Evans
Telephone: 617-896-3111
Rooms: 6, all share bathroom facilities.
Rates: In season, single, $12, double, $18. Off season: single, $10, double $15.
Facilities: Open all year, closed for meals on Mondays. During off season, meals on weekends and on request. TV in lounge. Parking.

HOW TO GET THERE:

Route 6A and Tubman Road, at Brewster, Cape Cod, Massachusetts.

Housed in an 1828 building that was once a church, The Inn of the Golden Ox is run by a man who used to be an Episcopal minister, until he lost his voice. It is coming back, and when you meet Charles Evans, half German, a quarter Swiss and a quarter Welsh, you feel that somehow, the right thing has happened. A giant of a man, Mr. Evans welcomes you to his Inn.

The Inn is small, charmingly decorated, red and white checked tablecloths for luncheon, something more formal for night time. The menu, written on blackboards, is German. Not all wurst and kraut, but truly *beautiful* German cooking. Good German beer is available, as well as a nice selection of wine.

The rooms for travelers are small, furnished with massive Victorian pieces, much like rooms in a small European inn.

E: I especially liked the wallpapers used throughout the Inn.

S: The imaginative, authentic German food proves everything I ever thought about German cuisine is wrong. The marinated lentils are delightful, and have you ever had stollen, all stuffed with citron, with a marzipan center? Come in the winter, around the holidays.

> *The crackle of an inn's hearth can melt the chilliest of minds and bodies.*

The Colonial Inn
Concord, Massachusetts
01742

Innkeeper: David S. Benoit
Telephone: 617-369-9200
Rooms: 60, all with bath, 20 old colonial rooms.
Rates: The Main Inn, EP $20 to $50. The John Keyes
House, housekeeping rooms, $196 and up per week.
$5 extra per person, per week. Crib or cot $3 extra.
Prescott wing $19-$25.
Facilities: Large public dining room, Village Forge Bar.
Small rooms for private parties. Parking. Open all
year.

HOW TO GET THERE:
Located on Route 2, west from Mass. 128, 18 miles
from Boston, 215 miles from New York.

Only minutes from Electronics Row (Route 128) the green at Concord has changed little in the last 200 years. The Colonial Inn stands at the end of the green, waiting to welcome the traveller, be he tourist, businessman, or scholar come to pay tribute to great writers of the past, Emerson, Thoreau, Hawthorne, Alcott; they all lived here, in this little village.

Thoreau's family actually lived in the Inn, and there is a dining room now where he had his study. The oldest part of the Inn was built in 1716, and people have been adding to it ever since. There are many small private dining rooms, as well as a large dining room, that is presently being made even larger. The food has a real New England touch, with home baked goods a feature.

Many of the colonial rooms have wide board floors, beamed ceilings, and there is the dearest little bridal suite, all blue and white, that is said to be haunted. When Elizabeth slept there, the light over the bed came on at 3:00 a.m. An unseen hand? There is much to see in Historic Concord, "Here once the embattled farmers stood, And fired the shot heard 'round the world." Walden Pond is very much unchanged for the ecologists and nature lovers.

The Village Forge Bar has an ever growing collection of old farm implements hanging from the walls and ceiling. It's as pleasant a place to have a drink as you'll find in a long day's journey.

E: Right in the Inn, and nearby are some lovely shops with quaint old things and lovely new ones.

S: Mad for history and literature as I am, I go quietly ape in this beautiful old town. In this rapidly changing world it is so rare to find that things are still the same "under the lilacs."

Deerfield Inn
Deerfield, Massachusetts
01342

Innkeeper: George W. Butler
Telephone: 413-774-3147
Rooms: 12 with bath.
Rates: Single, $18; Double, $24–$28.
Facilities: Air conditioned dining room serving Breakfast, Lunch and Dinner. Cocktail Lounge. Snack shop. Parking. Open all year except Christmas holiday. Rooms for private functions.

HOW TO GET THERE:

Exit 24 from I91, Exit 26 to Greenfield, then south on Route 10.

In a quiet village, that has been beautifully restored, near a major stream, surrounded by long views of the valley and wooded hills, the Deerfield Inn has been dispensing hospitality since it was built in 1884 to serve as a stagecoach stop.➤The dining room has been beautifully enlarged, with four magnificent bay windows that overlook the patio. Gleaming old silver, crystal chandeliers, mahogany chairs and lots of flowers give this charming room an ambiance you won't soon forget.➤After a drink or two in the new cocktail lounge, a delicious dinner in the dining room, any traveller is happy to go upstairs and sink into a fourposter bed, utterly relaxed.

On the same street as the Inn are the 18th Century Houses that have been restored, and are open to visitors all year. Deerfield Academy is located here, and there are five college campuses within a few minutes drive. Breakfast, Lunch and Dinner are served at this nice old Inn.

E: I could stay here forever.

S: The summer terrace is a peaceable retreat, especially when you have been "college shopping."

> *Modern man has done wonderous things in preserving the whooping cranes and country inns.*

Coonamessett Inn
Falmouth, Massachusetts
02541

Innkeeper: Terence P. Ryan
Telephone: 617-548-2300
Rooms: 3 double rooms in Inn, plus cottages. Baths to share.
Rates: Sept. 15–June 24, EP $8–$13 off season per person.
  June 25–September 15, double only, $18–$41.
Facilities: Open 7 days a week, all year. Breakfast, Lunch
  and Dinner. Bar. Parking.

HOW TO GET THERE:

Take Route 28 at the Bridge over the Canal, into
Falmouth. Turn left on Jones Road, and at the intersection of Gifford Street you will see the Inn.

Don't despair if you can't get a room in the Coona-messett Inn, ➤ the cottages are fine, especially good if you are traveling en masse (with the family). The grounds are beautiful, kept in mint condition, year round. We love the Cape off season, and it is good to know that no matter what day we decide to come, we will receive a cordial welcome here.

The food is excellent, a large, varied menu, served by friendly waitresses. Breakfasts are memorable. Lunch attracts a large group, this place is really well-known, and dinner is great, with lobster served four different ways. You can even have lobster sauce on your scrod. Meat eaters aren't forgotten either, and two favorites are featured, sweetbreads and bacon with sauce supreme, and a lamb chop mixed grill. ➤ Desserts have a menu all their own. Fantastic.

➤ Little shops to lure you, and all around the loveliest array of grass, trees, flowers, shrubs and peace, don't forget the peace.

E: I wish I lived closer, because I like the whole thing, starting with the Innkeeper, and continuing down the list.

S: The flower arrangements, fresh every other day, done by a man who really knows how to arrange.

> *The register of a country inn is a treasure of the names of good people.*

Whale Inn

Goshen, Massachusetts

01032

Innkeeper: Kenneth T. Walden
Telephone: 413-268-7246
Rooms: 5, plus 1 suite, all with private baths.
Rates: $18 double, $12 single.
Facilities: Large dining room, open all year except Christmas
Day. Bar. Breakfast, Lunch and Dinner served.
Parking. TV. Bedboard.

HOW TO GET THERE:

Exit I91 at Northampton, to Massachusetts Route 9.
The Inn is located on the right side of Main Street just
past the center of town.

The house that has been the Whale Inn for the past 50 years was built in 1799. There is a beehive fireplace behind the big guest room in the front of the house, hidden behind white panelling. "The Whale he swam around the ocean, and landed Jonah up in Goshen." The large dining room looks out over a lovely old-fashioned garden and lawn. English food is the mainstay of the menu.

Goshen is a small, quiet town, but on Friday and Saturday nights the Whale Inn really swings. There is a band, and dining and dancing are the order of the evening. So if you are seeking a quiet spot, plan to come on Monday through Thursday, or look up another quiet inn in this handy book.

The present owner is an engineer who tired of traveling, came home to Northampton, and bought the Whale seventeen years ago.

E: The charming tap room with ropes and stays welcomed me, and when I found the extra pillows on the comfortable beds, I refused to move another step.

S: The big, black ovens turn out delicious home baked goodies, and the roast beef is wonderful.

> *I can drink with a man who hates flowers, but if he has no appreciation of a good inn I cannot suffer him for a moment.*

The Fairfield Inn
Great Barrington, Massachusetts
01230

Innkeepers: Anne and Frank J. Hines
Telephone: 413-528-2720
Rooms: 11, all with bath.
Rates: May to October, Sunday to Friday, $25; Friday and
Saturday, $35. October to May, Sunday to Friday,
$25; Friday and Saturday, $28.
Facilities: Closed on Tuesday. Breakfast, Lunch and Dinner.
Bar. Parking. Restaurant accessible for wheelchair.
Tennis and Riding nearby. Golf. Swimming.

HOW TO GET THERE:
Just over the Connecticut line, where Route 7 meets
Route 23, on Route 41.

You are going to love this pretty place as much as we do. The spacious porches are shaded by ancient trees, the lawn slopes down to a brook complete with ducks. The rooms are immaculate, large and many of them have antique furnishings, including canopy beds. And the food! Did you ever have a fruit sandwich? Surprise yourself when you come here. There are quiches, and omelets, and also just plain hamburgers in case you are traveling with a young purist who will eat nothing else. The homemade breads wreak havoc with one's best laid diet plans, but they are too good to skip. The chef, who is a graduate of the Culinary Institute of America does not believe in dull foods.

Innkeeper Hines, a merry man, presides at the newly enlarged bar, and Mrs. Hines just seems to be everywhere, lending a hand in the kitchen, welcoming guests, keeping an eye on things. There are four daughters of the house, who according to their father, "got them into the Inn business."

Be sure to reserve, because this place is at the gateway to the Berkshires, and you know what summer is like up there.

Innkeeping takes twenty-five hours of every twenty-four, but done right it makes a wonderful life.

Country Inn
Harwichport, Massachusetts
02646

Innkeepers: Bill and Bernice Flynn
Telephone: 617-432-2769
Rooms: 8 rooms, 2 without bath.
Rates: Off season, per person, with bath, $9; near bath, $7, extra bed, $4. Friday before Memorial Day, through Labor Day, with bath, $11; near bath, $8, extra bed, $5.
Facilities: Breakfast (for house guests) no lunch, Dinner by reservation for transients. Bar in the lounge. Private dining room for small parties.

HOW TO.GET THERE:

Follow Route 6, the Mid-Cape Highway to Exit 10, Harwich. Go right on Route 124 (Pleasant Lake Avenue). Cross Main Street in Harwich and continue on Routes 124 and 39 (Sisson Road) to the Inn.

Country Inn is its name, and it is perfect. Covered with rambler roses, centrally located on the Cape, it sits by the side of the road, waiting to welcome you. A lovely old Cape home on ten acres, Country Inn makes a fine homebase for exploring the Cape. ☛ There are 11 fireplaces in this 200 year old house. There are also three new tennis courts for the tennis buffs among us.

There are a couple of bedrooms on the first floor, so if you are travelling in a wheelchair, it is possible to stay here. There is ☛ only one sitting at dinner, served from 6:30 to 8:30, in a dining room that is noted for its sunsets. Wine is available by the carafe, and there is a modest wine list.

Mr. Flynn, who is the chef, believes in breakfast. Eggs Benedict are a speciality and the ham and cheese omelets are delicious, light and fluffy.

&: I particularly like this Inn's name. The spinet piano in the lounge invites the guests to tinkle a tune.

S: Down toward the center of town is a devilishly attractive shop called "Traveling Kitty." Don't miss it.

The time between sunset and the completeness of night should be spent around a well laid board with assurances of a warm bed to follow.

The Gateways
Lenox, Massachusetts
01240

Innkeepers: Mr. and Mrs. Dan Browne
Telephone: 413-637-2532
Rooms: 14, doubles all have private bath, singles share.
Rates: Double: Summer $42; Winter $28.
Facilities: Open all year for house guests except Christmas.
Dining room closed Monday and Tuesday. Continental breakfast for house guests included in price
of room. Lunch served for house guests or private
parties. Bar. Parking. Television. 1 room accessible
for wheelchair. 1½ miles to Tanglewood.

HOW TO GET THERE:
71 Walker Street, right on Route 7A and 183 on the
right-hand side going north.

The Gateways began life as a mansion, built for Mr. Procter, the Ivory Soap magnate, in the shape of a cake of his favorite product, square, and flat topped. Mr. and Mrs. Dan Browne, having been in the food business all their lives, decided they wanted to get away from the hurly-burly life on Long Island and run a country inn. Several years ago they located this roomy old house in Lenox. The day we were there they had just received a beautifully penned note describing a room occupied the previous week as a "Corner of Heaven." The massive old furniture looks so right in the high ceilinged rooms. The dining room furniture, and the things in the bar, come from a furniture factory owned by the Brownes. Come to stay and do your shopping.

Mr. Browne is very, very particular about his kitchen, it is, like Ivory Soap, 99 and 44/100% pure. There is a pre-concert dinner, as well as more leisurely dining. The food is imaginative and excellent.

E: Breakfast on the garden terrace beneath a yellow and white striped awning is my idea of the way to begin a summer day.

S: The oval windows beside the front door, and the stairway (attributed to Stanford White) are beautiful.

The Village Inn
Lenox, Massachusetts
01240

Innkeepers: Richard and Marie Judd
Telephone: 413-637-0020
Rooms: 26 rooms, 15 baths.
Rates: Double room: $19, winter, $24 in fall and early summer, $29-$39 in summer. Rooms without private bath deduct $3, and $4 is deducted for single occupancy. Summer week-ends 3 night minimum with check in advance, plus 5.7% tax.
Facilities: Open all year. Breakfast, Lunch and Dinner. Bar. Parking. Television.

HOW TO GET THERE:
3 hours by car from New York, via Taconic Parkway, 2 hours from Boston, exit 2 from Mass. Turnpike. Or take Greyhound Bus.

25 years as an insurance man in New York has prepared Richard Judd for running a country inn. He really *cares* about people. The 200-year-old house has been operated as an inn for about 150 years. If these old walls could talk . . . hand-hewn trees of stout size, fastened with wooden pegs support its roofs and floors. Attics abound with ancient trunks, valises and dusty hat boxes filled with antique possessions of guests, innkeepers and their employees. Come for a night, a month, or the rest of your life. There is a cordial welcome for music lovers, antique seekers, and country inn buffs.

Poor Richard's Pub, built in the old cellars, furnished with seats made from church pews, stained glass, a wall aquarium, and a tool collection from the past, opens at 11:30 A.M. (1:30 on Sunday) to serve drinks and hot sandwiches until late evening. There is a cozy corner for lovers, and in winter a bright fire to warm your bones.

There's so much to do in this quaint old town, or near it. Not far away is the studio of the great sculptor, Daniel Chester French. (The Lincoln Memorial is his work.) The Williamstown Theater and the Clark Art Museum are a short drive up Route 7. Norman Rockwell's collected works can be seen in the Corner House Museum in nearby Stockbridge. Dance at Jacob's Pillow and classical music at Tanglewood are world famous.

E: Poor Richard's Pub is my place, and this is the only Inn I know that serves Irish Coffee for breakfast every day.

S: The lovely organ in the parlor, and the Innkeeper who plays it are part of the charm of The Village Inn.

Jared Coffin House
Nantucket, Massachusetts
02554

Innkeeper: Philip Whitney Read
Telephone: 617-228-2400
Rooms: 41 rooms, 13 in main house, 16 simpler rooms in
Eben Allen Wing, and 12 rooms in the Daniel Web-
ster House, across the patio.
Rates: Main House; $36–$45. Later Additions; $16–$36.
Facilities: Dining Room, Eben Allen Room for private
parties, The Tap Room, Patio for summer luncheon.

HOW TO GET THERE:

By ferry from Woods Hole. (Call 617-548-5011 for
reservations on ferry.) Summer ferry from Hyannis.
Airplane from Boston, Hyannis or New York. The
House is located 2 blocks north of Main Street, 2
blocks west of Steamboat Wharf.

It's well worth the 30 mile trip by ferry, or a plane trip from Boston or New York, to end your journey at the Jared Coffin House in Nantucket, Massachusetts. Built as a private house in 1845, the three story brick house with its slate roof, became an inn only 12 years later. In 1961 the Nantucket Historic Trust purchased the house, and two years were spent restoring the main house, the addition, and the adjoining house to the original style and architecture. Nantucket Island has become the center for a revival of needlework unprecedented anywhere else in the country, and perhaps the world. Six thousand yards of material was made to use in the Guest Rooms of the Jared Coffin House. The spirit and feeling of the glorious days of Nantucket's brief reign as queen of the world's whaling ports remains in the lovely Inn.

The Tap Room, located on the lowest level, is a warm happy room. Breakfast and Lunch are served there daily. The main dining room, papered with authentic period paper, is quiet and elegant. Spode Lowestoft china and pistol handled silverware reflect the good life demanded by the 19th century owners of the great whaling ships.

The Inn is located in the heart of Nantucket's Historic District, only an eighth of a mile from a public beach, a mile from the largest public beach and tennis courts, and a pleasant three mile bicycle ride from superb surf swimming on the South Shore.

E: Chef Elliot Norton is a wizard with the really fine food.

S: The size and the quantity of the luxurious bath towels pleased me greatly. The housekeeping staff does a wonderful job, and the exquisite antiques reflect their loving care.

The Flying Cloud Inn

New Marlboro, Massachusetts
01230

Innkeepers: Martin and Beverly Langeveld

Telephone: 413-229-2113

Rooms: 8 with bath; 2 that share.

Rates: MAP $38 per person per day, double room includes gratuity. Double room with shared bath, $33 per person.

Facilities: Open May 7 to October 31, Thanksgiving weekend, and December 15 to March 21. Bar, Breakfast, Lunch on request and Dinner. Cross-country skiing, snow shoeing, sleds and toboggans. Clay tennis court and an all-weather composition court. Swimming in a spring fed pond.

HOW TO GET THERE:

From New York and south take 684 to 84 east to Connecticut 8. North to 44 west to 183 north, then 14.5 miles to the Inn. From Boston and east, take the Mass. Pike to exit 2. Then go 102 to 7 south to 23 east to 57. Beyond New Marlboro, you fork right off 57 (Sandisfield State Forest), 2 miles to the Inn. Via Hartford 44 west to 183 north.

The Flying Cloud is ready for you any season of the year. There are 200 acres of lawns, meadows and woodland, abounding with wildflowers, birds and friendly animals. Summer there is a tennis pro teaching on the two courts. One is clay, one is all-weather, both are carefully tended. The well-manicured lawns provide croquet, badminton, volleyball and room to practice short golf shots.

The Inn accommodates only 20 people at a time, so if you want to be alone there is plenty of room for you to do so. Seclusion can be beautiful in the proper places.

The rooms are very spacious and furnished with beautiful antiques. Most rooms have twin beds. There are no phone extensions or TVs in the rooms.

There is only one seating for dinner which allows it to be served at the peak of perfection. Menus feature fresh vegetables from the garden in the summer and fresh from a nearby market in winter. They are always testing new recipes in the kitchen.

The Inn is ideal for small meetings and seminars, or how about 10 couples taking over the whole Inn for a weekend? Sure could be alot of fun.

They have a Golden Retriever called Sundance, who will walk with you, and two great young people, the Innkeepers, to really coddle you.

E: The wine cellar is superb. They have great wine tasting partys. Call and they will arrange one for you.

S: The quiet and seclusion of this countryside move me.

A warming fire, a strong drink, a genial innkeeper . . . and winter is somewhere in the hills but is not here.

Old Farm Inn
Pigeon Cove, Massachusetts
01966

Innkeepers: The Balzarini Family
Telephone: 617-546-3237
Rooms: 6, 4 with bath, 2 rooms share.
Rates: July, August and September $18 double occupancy. October through June, $14. Rooms with connecting kitchen, $24 each, off season, $20. Open all year.
Facilities: Open all winter for rooms. Luncheon and Dinner served from early spring to late fall. No bar. (Rockport is dry but set-ups are provided.) Outdoor dining terrace. Special Sunday morning Brunch.

HOW TO GET THERE:
Follow Route 127 from the center of Rockport for 2 miles to Halibut Point.

At the northern most tip of Cape Ann is a dear little Inn being happily run by an entire family. This salt water farm has been there since 1705, and the present house is thought to date to 1799. The barn has been renovated to a small guest house. Reservations are a must as this is just a little Inn. During good weather, there is dining on the screened garden terrace.

Everyone in the family has a specialty; each specialty gives something to the whole picture. When we walked into the kitchen late one spring morning, one aunt was stirring the Indian Pudding cooking in the old black iron wood stove, another aunt was fixing salad. An uncle had just delivered a 40 pound halibut, and Mrs. Balzarini was preparing the dining room for luncheon. The son of the house was conducting our tour, and he added "My father makes a mean duck!"

E: He's absolutely right! Crisp duckling is a favorite of mine and I always order it here.

S: I was beguiled with the antique cradle on the hearth, as well as the other antiques.

I was lost, I was tired, and I was discouraged, and then I found a friendly inn.

Bradford Gardens Inn
Provincetown, Massachusetts
02657

Innkeepers: John Venner and James Logan
Telephone: 617-487-1616
Rooms: 8, all with bath. 6 with working fireplaces.
Rates: Year-round rates from $27 to $60. Studio apartment
that belonged to artists Frederick Waugh and Hans
Hofman $60 a day—sleeps 6 and has a full kitchen.
Penthouse—$60 a day.
Facilities: Open all year. Only one meal is served, Brunch
until nearly noon, except light breakfast in July—
August. Some rooms have color TV. There is one
room across the street from the main Inn that is
suitable for a wheelchair. Lovely garden.

HOW TO GET THERE:
Mid-Cape Highway to Provincetown. 177 Bradford
Street. The bus from New York will stop at the door.
The Innkeeper will pick up guests at the Provincetown
airport gratis.

How rare the inn that lets you have a fire in your bedroom fireplace, and furnishes the wood to burn in it. Bradford Gardens, one of the few places in this far-out spot to stay open all year, is a cozy spot, even on a blizzardy winter day. If you like roses, come in the middle of May, when the hundreds of rose bushes in the garden burst into bloom, and the Japanese cherry tree showers its wealth of blossoms over the terrace.

The only meal served at the Inn is a fabulous brunch, Eggs Portuguese, Quiche Lorraine, Eggs Franciscan. Stay for a week and you will never be served the same thing twice. The owners recommend the Landmark Inn and the Red Inn for dinner, both open all year.

Bradford Gardens is within strolling distance of the main part of Provincetown. Out there at the tip of the Cape you are never far from the ocean or bay. The Inn has no bar, so bring your own whatever.

It is sometimes possible to rent the artist's studio for as little as one night. It is charming, constructed entirely of lumber from shipwrecks that took place 200 years ago. It has a gigantic fireplace, two bedrooms, one in a loft, a full kitchen with a dishwasher and ice maker, a dining area and an unbelievable living room. Or try the Penthouse, it has a fantastic harbor view.

Bikes are preferred transportation in P-town, and can be rented. If you are tired of the motel life, hide away on Bradford Street, on Cricket Hill.

E: Suzy and I are the greatest beachcombers around, and the beaches out here are great.

S: Constant improvement is the off-season activity for the owners. Be sure to call for a reservation, the Innkeepers sometimes go inn-creeping.

The Yankee Clipper
Rockport, Massachusetts
01966

Innkeeper: Frederick Wemyss (pronounced Weems)
Telephone: 617-546-3407
Rooms: 26, most with private bath, except for suites. Some air conditioned.
Rates: The Inn, July 1 through Labor Day, AP: $53–$66; extra person in suite $22. 5% discount by the month. Spring and Fall, May 15 to June 30, Sept 5 to Oct. 15, MAP (breakfast and dinner), $42–$56, extra person in suite $20. 5% discount by week. Rates on application.

Facilities: 3 separate buildings in beautiful gardens. Private and public sun decks. Dining terrace. Heated ▬salt water pool. Color TV in lounge. No Bar.

HOW TO GET THERE:
Route 128 North and east to Cape Ann. 128 intersects route 127 at 2 points, and you can reach the Clipper by turning left at either one. The second one is the shorter. After taking the second one, go about 4 miles to the "corners" where you should see the sign for the Inn.

In early June the pale pink poppies are as big as luncheon plates, nodding beside the lupin, looking over rockbound Sandy Bay. Peace, loving kindness from the Wemyss family, and perfect surroundings are the main characteristics of the Yankee Clipper Inn. The rooms are named for the famous old ships. Whether you stay at the Inn, or The Quarterdeck (where the whole front wall is glass, looking over a perennial border to the water) or at the Bulfinch House across the street, you will be supremely comfortable. Swim in the salt water pool or dive from the rocks into Sandy Bay, sit dozing over your book on a secluded deck, or meander downtown to see the wonderful shops and art galleries of Rockport.

The menu is limited, and delicious, you decide early in the day what you will have for dinner's main course. If it's off season, Mr. Wemyss just might make blueberry pancakes for breakfast! Luncheon on the terrace is delightful.

Remember that Rockport is DRY, and you will have to bring your own. No wine or whiskey can be served in the dining room. If the Inn is not serving lunch, there are several excellent places nearby to eat, Old Farm Inn, Peg Leg, Oleanna's and Sea Shell. If weather conditions are right, you can enjoy a sightseeing trip on Mr. Wemyss' boat at no extra charge, or a sauna and whirlpool at a nominal fee.

There are books all over the Inn, places to play games, places just for sitting and contemplating.

E: I want a permanent reservation for the room with the sleigh beds on the third floor, the one with the deck.

S: Would that I could be marooned at the Inn, all those lovely books to read, all that lovely music on the hi-fi, those lovely rocks to look at, all the peace and quietude, plus the flowers!

Inn For All Seasons

Scituate, Massachusetts

02066

Innkeepers: Dorothy, Stan, Elaine and Ed Wondolowski, and Joshua the dog.
Telephone: 617-545-6699
Rooms: 8, no private baths. Share 2 large ones.
Rates: June 15 to Sept. 15, single $20–$26, double $26–$32. Sept. 16 to June 14, single $13–$19, double $18–$24.
Facilities: Continental Breakfast during the week. Sunday Brunch. Lunch and Dinner—Tuesday through Sunday. Closed Monday for food. No Bar. B.Y.O.

HOW TO GET THERE:

32 Barker Road overlooks Scituate Harbor. Barker Road is off of Jericho Road, just opposite the state public boat launching area. From Boston take Southeast Expressway south to Rt. 3. Continue south to Exit 31. Turn left at bottom of ramp and take right onto Rt. 123 at traffic light. Go 8 miles to traffic lights intersecting Rt. 3A and turn left. Go 2 miles and turn right at town hall. Turn left at 3rd traffic light onto Jericho Rd. Take 2nd left after Pier 44 onto Barker Rd. 2 blocks up on right.

A delightful surprise brimming over with tender loving care, great ambience, and a marvelous bunch of Wondolowskis. They have taken over the old Craig House Inn, and money aside, have poured hours upon hours of their own time to create a Victorian country inn furnished to that great queen's taste.

An inn since 1921, the Inn For All Seasons has never seen a better time. The rooms, though none with bath, do have running water, and all are named and named well: Wicker, Gold, Red, Tapestry, Patchwork, and Pine. Immaculately clean and furnished in fine antiques. The parlor with a huge hand-carved mantel is a perfect spot before and after dinner. While at the moment there is no liquor license, wine is being planned, and if the patrons and the neighbors of historic Scituate wish it, libations will follow. For the nonce, you are urged to bring your own, but you might check the situation when you make a reservation.

The kitchen has a rule that should be in every kitchen, all vegetables and fruits are fresh. The two dining rooms are correctly small with the formal one boasting two brass balloon chandeliers.

With the history of Scituate around you, a functioning lighthouse with live-in light keepers, and a working fishing fleet, this is a great hideaway for fishing, swimming, or best of all (and in spite of its proximity to Plymouth Rock) a great spot for plain, non-puritanical loafing. Come for six days, and there is no charge for the seventh.

E: Wicker, wicker, everywhere, some antique, some just wicker and all just wonderful.

S: The beds are so comfortable and the towels are plentiful.

The Red Lion Inn
Stockbridge, Massachusetts
01262

Innkeeper: Henricus G. A. Bergmans

Telephone: 413-298-5545

Rooms: 100, 65 with bath, others running water only, all air conditioned. 24 rooms with TV.

Rates: Nov. 1 thru April 30: Single, $14–$20; Double, $24–$28. May 1 thru Oct. 31: Single, $18–$24; Double, $28–$32. July 1 thru August 31: Single, $24–$36; Double, $32–$48. Additional person $6–$16. A minimum stay of 2 days is required on weekends during July–August. Advance deposit of the full daily rate is required.

Facilities: Open all year. Parking. 24 hour switchboard. Elevator. Ramp for wheelchair. Swimming pool. Outdoor patio. Bar. Breakfast, Lunch and Dinner.

HOW TO GET THERE:

By car: Stockbridge is 3 hours from New York, 2½ hours from Boston, 1 hour from Albany. Exit 2 on Massachusetts Turnpike. US Route 7.

For 200 years there has been an inn in Stockbridge serving travellers, famous and unknown. Called the Red Lion Inn since 1900, this large white house is being refurbished and polished with loving care by Jack and Jane Fitzpatrick, the present owners. Capably managed for them by Henricus G. A. Bergmans, an amiable Dutchman, the Inn is the center of much activity on the main street of Stockbridge. There are brass beds, fourposters with canopies, rocking chairs covered to match the colonial prints of the wallpapers, a marvelous elevator, recently renovated. A large collection of antique China teapots lines the beams of the main parlor, antique keys hang from the mantle, oriental rugs warm the floors, and the old pewter gleams from the corner cupboard. A cat named Gus patrols the premises.

The food served in the main dining room is especially good, prepared in a newly renovated kitchen by expert hands, and the drinks served in Widow Bingham's Tavern are delicious. Homemade pie ends a menu that is sophisticated with a country air. The wine list is good, ranging from Chateau Mouton Rothchild to a New York Chablis.

Within strolling distance of the Inn are antique shops, boutiques, art galleries and museums. The Corner House, a charming 18th century home is a museum containing a collection of paintings by Norman Rockwell, a local resident. A dollhouse and a roomful of antique dolls make this a delightful place to spend an hour or so.

Golf, tennis and swimming (Inn's own heated pool) are available. Skiing in winter, hockey games, springtime walks, autumn foliage, Pleasant Valley Bird Sanctuary, music at Tanglewood, dance at Jacob's Pillow, and every evening at sunset from "apple blossom time until frost" the children's chimes are played from the Children's Chime Tower erected by David Dudley Field in 1878, as a memorial to his grandchildren.

Publick House
Sturbridge, Massachusetts
01566

Innkeeper: Buddy Adler
Telephone: 617-347-3313
Rooms: 21 rooms, air conditioned, all with private baths and complimentary Continental Breakfast. Col. Ebenezer Crafts House—9 rooms, swimming pool and 50 acres, 1⅓ mile from Publick House.
Rates: $24 to $26.
Facilities: Open all year. Telephone switchboard. Lunch and Dinner served. Bar. Piano player in Tavern. TV in lounge. No elevator, but ramp to restaurant. Gift Shop.

HOW TO GET THERE:

Massachusetts Turnpike to Exit 9. The Publick House is located on the Common at Sturbridge, on Route 131. From Hartford, take I-84. It becomes I-86 and brings you right into Sturbridge. Take Exit 3.

Very little has changed at the Publick House in the last 200 years, the green still stretches along in front of it, the trees still cast their welcome shade. Not far away ➤Old Sturbridge Village has been assembled and restored, a living museum of the past. The Publick House is still taking care of the wayfarer, feeding him well, providing a bed, supplying robust drink. Many of the old practices and celebrations have been revived, the Boar's Head Procession during the Christmas holidays is one. They *do* keep Christmas at the Publick House! All twelve days. ➤Winter weekends are times for special treats, chestnuts roasting by an open fire, sleigh rides through Old Sturbridge Village, a happy step backward in time.

Twenty-one guest rooms have been decorated with period furniture, and the wide floor boards and beamed ceilings have been here since Colonel Ebenezer Crafts founded the Inn in 1771. The barn, connected to the main house with a ramp, has been transformed into a restaurant. Double doors, topped by a glorious Sunburst window lead into a restaurant that serves delectable goodies. There is a little musician's gallery overlooking the main dining room, that is still divided into stalls. Beneath this is an attractive tap room, where a pianist holds forth, tinkling out nice noises.

A blueberry patch, and garden which covers more than an acre of land, provide the Inn with fresh fruit and vegetables during the summer.

&: Way on top of the Inn is a suite called the Penthouse. The view from these rooms in the very early spring of the Common through the feathery new leaves of April is enough to bring me back from the far corners of the earth.

S: I found my way (by following my nose) around behind the Inn to the Bake Shop, where every day fresh banana bread, sticky-buns, deep dish apple pies, corn bread and muffins come out of the ovens to tempt us from our diets! Take some along, in case of hunger pangs along the road.

Longfellow's Wayside Inn
Sudbury, Massachusetts
01776

Innkeeper: Francis J. Koppeis
Telephone: 617-443-8846
Rooms: 10 air conditioned rooms with private bath.
Rates: Single $16, Double $20, plus tax.
Facilities: Telephones in 9 of the 10 rooms. No TV. Bar. Dining room. Breakfast, Lunch and Dinner. Horses boarded. Pets limited. No room service.

HOW TO GET THERE:

From Boston: Take Mass. Pike to Route 128, North to Route 20, Exit 49-west. Coming from New York, take Massachusetts Pike to Route 495 to Route 20, East.

Eight generations of travellers have found food and lodging for "man and beast" at the Wayside Inn. Route 20 is the old stagecoach road to Boston, now well off the beaten track, but you will find the Inn looking much the same as it has for over 270 years, still dispensing hearty food and drink, and supplying a few comfortable beds. In early times people on the road slept five or six to a room, but now the rooms with twin beds and private baths are limited to two.

In 1955 the Inn was partially destroyed by fire but the older part was saved, and when the restoration was done, many things were put back the way they were in the beginning, and many 19th century "improvements" were changed. Part of the Inn serves as a museum, with priceless antiques displayed in their original setting.

There is a large dining room, a bar, a tiny gift shop, and a lovely walled garden. At the end of the garden path is a bust of Henry Wadsworth Longfellow who was inspired by the Inn to link together a group of poems, in the fashion of The Canterbury Tales. The Landlord's Tale is known to us all as Paul Revere's Ride.

Henry Ford bought 5000 acres surrounding the Inn in 1925, and since then this historic spot has been preserved for generations yet to come. A little way up the road stands a lovely chapel, the little red school house that gained fame in "Mary Had a Little Lamb," and a stone Grist Mill, that still grinds grain for the rolls and muffins baked at the Inn. ◀ In the summer vegetables served at the Inn are locally grown.

E: The waterfall at the Grist Mill really flipped me. The stone work is unbelievable!

S: After trying a "Stonewall" cocktail, a gin drink, I submit that it is *the* Revolutionary cocktail, and subsided quietly into my Indian Pudding, a favorite dessert.

LE JARDIN, WILLIAMSTOWN, MASSACHUSETTS

Le Jardin
Williamstown, Massachusetts
01267

Innkeeper: Walter Hayn
Telephone: 413-458-8032
Rooms: 9, 8 baths.
Rates: $16 single to $24 double.
Facilities: Open all year. Closed Tuesday for dinner. Breakfast served June 1, complimentary for house guests in off season. Lunch served starting May 1. Dinner. Bar. Parking.

HOW TO GET THERE: Routes 2 and 7, Williamstown. South of town, on the right.

Hemlock Brook burbles past the sugar maples and you find yourself in a comfortable, unpretentious country inn. The owner-manager is the chef, has been a chef for 16 years, but is happy to have the advice of his business associates the Grosso family, who are running a larger operation just down the road a bit.

The menu is more than a little French, translated nicely into the language of the country. The essence of good food is time, but even the hasty diner is taken care of here with steaks and chops. We love to linger, sampling les hors d'oeuvres and les potages, while the baby pheasant simmers in cognac, or the sweetbreads sauté in black butter. We throw caloric caution to the winds and order Poire Hélène, or sample some cheese from the cheese board. The Sunday Brunch offered at Le Jardin is an extravaganza of good things to eat. It begins at 10:30, which strikes us as only sensible.

The old-fashioned rooms are comfortable, nothing fancy, but a more than adequate place to spend the night.

&: This Innkeeper makes his own maple syrup. In early spring all the maples are festooned with little pots, and in the kitchen there is a huge pot simmering on the back of the stove boiling down the sap. Massachusetts Maple Syrup.

S: An artistic arrangement of bread, all kinds, all shapes, all sizes, caught my eye. The work of the chef, of course.

Old Yarmouth Inn

Yarmouth Port, Massachusetts

02675

Innkeeper: Shane E. Peros
Telephone: 617-362-3191
Rooms: 12, all with a private bath.
Rates: Inquire for seasonal rates.
Facilities: Lunch and Dinner. Closed on Mondays, October
15–June 1. Bar. Parking. TV.

HOW TO GET THERE:

Leave Route 6 (Mid-Cape Highway) at Yarmouth
Port exit to Route 6A, one right turn, and one mile will
bring you to the Old Yarmouth Inn.

The Old Yarmouth Inn is the oldest Inn on Cape Cod, built in 1696 as a Wayside Staging Inn, there have been many owners, but it maintains its charm. The building sags a bit, and when you come in it is like savoring a bit of yesterday, old leather suitcases, quaint papered hat boxes, dusty coats, hobnail boots, ancient horse brasses, all combine to carry you back to the olden days.

There is salt air here, flowers, sunshine, somedays a little fog. You can dine indoors or out at The Old Yarmouth Inn, sea food is, of course, a specialty of the house. Vegetables, salads, and herbs come fresh from the garden, flaky pastries, rich cakes and hot breads burst from the ovens.

You are only four miles from the famous Cape Playhouse at Dennis, one of the original "straw hat" theaters. There are several fine beaches near by, fishing, boating and day trips to Nantucket and Martha's Vineyard can be arranged.

E: The antique bug is gonna bite me, sure's I live if I keep coming back to Yarmouth Port.

S: I love their attitude about roast beef: "Our prime beef is cooked medium to rare and we cannot accept responsibility for well done meat." Amen.

ARLINGTON INN

Arlington Inn
Arlington, Vermont
05250

Innkeepers: Amy and Stephen Lundy
Telephone: 802-375-6532
Rooms: 12, 2 efficiency apartments, all with bath.
Rates: $25 for 2 with Continental Breakfast.
Facilities: The Inn is closed in April and November, and
    also Tuesday. Lunch and Dinner served. Bar. Parking.

HOW TO GET THERE:
    The Inn is located directly on Route 7, in the middle
    of Arlington.

84

It pleases us so much to see these young, new Innkeepers hard at work restoring their beautiful Greek Revival House to its former elegance. The house was built in 1848 by a man named Martin Chester Deming. The bar, in the house, is called the Deming Tavern, although the original tavern, owned by this man's family was across the street.

Amy is a weaver, and some of her very special work is displayed on the walls. Stephen is a man for all seasons, as what innkeeper cannot help but be. But he is a most gracious host, and we wish we could have tarried longer at this lovely spot. The food is excellent, ☛ purchased with care, prepared thoughtfully, and well presented.

S: I'm the lady who likes veal, and they do it well here.

A good innkeeper, a good cook, and an affable barkeeper are as standard in a country inn as a fire engine in a fire house.

The Brandon Inn
Brandon, Vermont
05733

Innkeepers: Trudy and Al Mitroff, and family
Telephone: 802-247-5766
Rooms: 60, 48 with private baths, others connecting baths. All sprinkler protected.
Rates: Rate schedule is complicated because European Plan, Modified American Plan and Full American Plan are all offered. Prices range from $18 up single EP, to $30 up per person full AP. Double $24 up EP or AP. Suggest you write for schedule.
Facilities: Open all year. Breakfast, Lunch and Dinner. Bar. Elevator. Ample parking. 40 air conditioned rooms. TV. Swimming pool.

HOW TO GET THERE:
Brandon is located on Rte. US 7 and Vermont Rte. 73, on the village green, 16 miles north of Rutland. 3½ hours drive from Boston, 5¼ from NYC and 3 from Montreal. Greyhound and Vermont Rapid Transit Buses stop in Brandon; air service to Burlington or Rutland; Amtrack to Essex Junction or White River Junction.

Your host at the Brandon Inn, famed as a hostelry since 1786, finds no language barrier with his guests; ➤ Al Mitroff speaks *nine* languages! This charming Czech (born though he was in Trenton, N.J.) brings a continental flavor to an old colonial inn. More than 40 years ago he was a busboy at the old Waldorf-Astoria, from there to the St. Regis, thence to the 1939 World's Fair in New York. Although he already had a degree in Physical Education from Columbia, Al then went to Cornell to learn the hotel business. It is a *pleasure* to stay at the Brandon Inn.

The rooms are large, some of them weren't large enough to suit our host, so he made one large room where two were before. These are rooms in the back of the Inn that used to be used for the coachmen, and are prized today because they are away from the road. The public rooms are charming, there are ➤ two enormous Pier Mirrors in the old parlor that must be priceless.

A filtered, crystal clear swimming pool, shuffle board, chip and putt green, croquet, fishing brook with an old mill dam, and easy interesting walks from the Inn, provide the guest with a melange of things to do. Four golf courses are a 5 to 20 minute drive. Nine major downhill ski areas are within a 10 to 45 minute drive, and two cross country ski areas are within a 10 minute drive.

The gardens behind the Inn, and the swimming pool, are lovely. The food is good, served by friendly ladies. ➤ When the wine we chose proved to be unavailable, Al Mitroff came himself with an especially chosen bottle for our pleasure. ➤ The Inn has been enshrined in the distinguished Historic Sites Register.

The Inn at *Mt. Ascutney*
Brownsville, Vermont
05037

Innkeeper: Daphne Henderson
Telephone: 802-484-5997
Rooms: 6 rooms, no private baths, but 2 tub-shower rooms
plus 3 powder rooms.
Rates: Bed and breakfast, $12 per person, double; $14,
single.
Facilities: Closed last 2 weeks in April, and last 2 weeks in
November. Lunch, Thursday through Sunday, June–
October. Breakfast for house guests. Dinner every
night but Wednesday. Bar. Television. Parking.
Cross-country skiing, Tennis. Riding.

HOW TO GET THERE:
Exit 8 from I91 northbound (Ascutney-Windsor) or
Exit 9 Southbound. Rte. 5 north 1 mile to Ascutney
State Park Rd. on left, to Rte. 44. Turn left and go 4
miles to Brownsville. The Inn is on Brook Road, look
for signs.

The house has been on this hilltop for about 150 years. Daphne Henderson, a charming blonde English lady has been there for only a short time, but her influence has already been felt. ➤ Whatever the season this house has to have one of the most spectacular views in the Green Mountains. There is always a breeze in summer, and a new flagstone terrace for dining and sitting. What more can you want? Well, country cooking, with a sophisticated touch.

Brownsville isn't really very far away from anywhere . . . Woodstock, Springfield and it is right at the foot of Mt. Ascutney. Summer theater at Weston is 45 minutes away. Curl up in front of the fire with a book about England or have a drink in the tiny English bar. There are three resident Henderson youngsters, (the oldest is in England), so there is plenty of action. Daphne came up the hill by way of Simsbury, Connecticut, to fulfill her dream of a real country inn.

E: Winter days when I feel lazy I like to watch the skiers on the slopes, which I can do without setting foot outside the Inn.

S: This is the little Inn where the kitchen is in the dining room, or the dining room is in the kitchen, depending entirely upon where you are standing. ➤ Last time I was there a great batch of blueberry muffins had just emerged from the oven. Goodbye diet.

Chester Inn
Chester, Vermont
05143

Innkeepers: Tom and Betsy Guido

Telephone: 802-875-2444

Rooms: 35 with bath.

Rates: Single $13–$19. Double $20–$28. Connecting rooms are available for families at a reduced rate. Rates include New England Country Breakfast. 10% Service Charge.

Facilities: Breakfast, house guests only. Lunch, Tuesday through Saturday. Dining room closed Monday. Dinner 6–8. Bar. Inn closed May & November.

HOW TO GET THERE:
From Route 91 take Route 103 to Chester. The Inn is on the Green.

When you arrive in Chester, you will find the Chester Inn gracing the Village Green. Walk up the steps onto the large porch with rocking chairs, and on through the door to the spacious living room with fireplace and great comfortable furniture. To the left, scout out the real ➤English pub. Pass through the door to the pool and patio area outside. Then pick a favorite spot, and rest a bit. The Iranian bird cage by the pool makes a charming planter.

There are seven skiing areas nearby, so for the skier who likes to ski a different area each day of the week, this is a logical place to lodge. After a day on the slopes, return to the Inn for a drink in the pub, a gourmet dinner, and then off to a snug bed. What more could you want? . . . well, on Saturdays there is a piano player for entertainment.

E: There is a shop connected to the Inn called "The Golden Pheasant" run by a very charming lady.

S: The spacious dining room has so much charm, and the heated swimming pool and two new all-weather tennis courts provide plenty of opportunity to exercise after that delicious gourmet dinner.

How good of you to have asked me in.

Independence Inn
Chester, Vermont
05143

Innkeepers: Dan and Jean, Sam and Delores
Telephone: 802-875-2525
Rooms: 8, 4 with bath
Rates: Double $16 with private bath. $14 share bath. Includes Continental Breakfast.
Facilities: Breakfast and Dinner served. Tuesday night buffet. Breakfast and Dinner served to guests of the Inn. Lounge. Open all year. Entertainment weekends.

HOW TO GET THERE:
Turn off Route 91 onto Route 103. Go to Chester and take Route 11w. to the Inn on the right.

Traveling down Route 11 one beautiful fall day, we came across this lovely old Inn that is a haven for anyone who wants to be in the country. The new owners are from Boston way, and have decided that Vermont offers more to both families. All the rooms have been freshly decorated with a true colonial feeling.

There is skiing all around the area, and upon your return to the Inn the dining room has a quaint old wood or coal burning stove with ▰▰ pots of steaming homemade soups. This is really worth getting cold for. The Inn has a huge lounge where they have lots of fun and music at times. The rooms are clean and ample.

E: Being an animal nut, I have a special affection for Dede, the inn beagle.

The cold, snowy enchantment of a New England winter is best viewed through the window of the barroom in a good inn.

Mountain Top Inn
Chittenden, Vermont
05737

Innkeeper: William P. Wolfe
Telephone: 802-483-2311
Rooms: 46, all with private bath.
Rates: $46–$64.
Facilities: Closed October 20–December 20 and April 1– May 28. Breakfast, Lunch optional, and Dinner served. Cocktail Lounge. Television. Dining room accessible to wheel chair. Parking. Swimming. Boating. Stables. Cross-country Skiing.

HOW TO GET THERE:
The Inn is 8 miles northeast of Rutland. Well-marked turnoffs are on Routes 7 and 4.

This spacious Inn was built in 1940 and 1941 around an old barn that was built in 1871. There are pictures showing the whole sequence in the lobby of the Inn. The township of Chittenden dates back to the 1790's and has been almost undisturbed during the passing years. The Inn really is on top of a mountain, 2000 feet up, overlooking the blue waters of Mountain Top Lake, which is really a power reservoir, and can be used for swimming and boating. You can even land your sea or ski plane on the lake, and that's something unusual, for sure.

Nothing has been overlooked for comfort and relaxation in this friendly spot. The snow in the immediate area is supposed to start earlier, last longer, and be deeper and better than anywhere in New England. ☛ The stables have a fine variety of ponies and horses, and you can take a ride in a surrey in summer, or a sleigh in winter. Bring your own horse, if you have one. He deserves a Vermont vacation, too.

The food is good, attractively served, with nice touches such as fresh raspberries on the fruit and cottage cheese plate.

E: I love the spectacular sun umbrellas designed by the Innkeeper. Traditional shapes kept blowing down the hill. These just whirl in the breeze.

S: Mrs. Wolfe's "folly," the stunning circular staircase that sweeps down from the lobby to the dining room, really caught my eye.

The Inn on the Common
Craftsbury Common, Vermont
05827

Innkeepers: Penny and Michael Schmitt
Telephone: 802-586-9619
Rates: MAP, $28 double; $34 single; children 25% less. Bed
    and Breakfast $19 double; $25 single; children 25%
    less.
Rooms: 6 guest bedrooms.
Facilities: Open all year, except November and April. Food
    and drinks served to house guests only. Tennis court.
    Croquet court. Cross-country skiing. Backgammon.
    Will open off season for private parties.

HOW TO GET THERE:

I–91 to St. Johnsbury, take Route 2 west and at West
Danville take 15 to Hardwick. Take Route 14 north to
Craftsbury, and continue north into the Common. The
Inn is on the left as you enter the village.

The word the Schmitt's like to use in describing their charming Inn on the Common is "unstuffy." The delicious meals are served around one large table. Young children, if any are staying at the Inn, dine an hour earlier, supervised by the teen-age daughter of the hosts. Fresh vegetables from the Inn garden, fresh flowers in all the bedrooms, are only some of the things that bring us back to our most northern Vermont Inn. Craftsbury Common is one of the loveliest villages in New England. It was founded in 1789, and many of the buildings date to the late 18th and early 19th centuries. Many of the original buildings are still standing. The village is spread out around a Common, an open fenced piece of land that is the center of much activity. The gardens of the houses built around the Common are old and charming. There is a farm in nearby Greensboro that is used for nature walks, hikes and picnics, up in the high hills, it has a breathtaking view. In addition to an excellent clay tennis court on the Inn grounds, nearby there are golf, swimming, sailing, canoeing, fishing, horseback riding, and skiing facilities during the winter. Chamber music concerts in the summer, and one wild night in late July when the Fiddler's Concert is held. Peace, quiet and beauty in copious amounts abound in this heavenly place. Be sure to reserve because there are only six bedrooms at the Inn.

E: All vegetables from their own garden is just something not to miss. The perennial beds are superb.

S: The summer soups, gazpacho, cucumber soup with onion, dill and cream, mint soup, avacado soup. All wonderful.

> *The good morning greeting and the good night good wish can only be found in a country inn.*

Barrows House

Dorset, Vermont

05251

Innkeepers: Charles and Marilyn Schubert
Telephone: 802-867-4455
Rooms: 26, nearly all private baths, a few share.
Rates: MAP Single, $22–$35, double $50–$60. Weekday luncheon extra.
Facilities: Open all year. Breakfast, Lunch and Dinner. Tavern. TV. Parking. Ski-touring. Fishing. Hunting. Outdoor heated swimming pool. Two outdoor tennis courts. Golf. Tennis. Sauna.

HOW TO GET THERE:
Take Exit 2—Brattleboro—off Interstate 91. Follow Route 30 North to South Londonderry (Rawsonville). The Inn is on your left, on Route 30, just beyond where Route 100 turns North.

Barrows House has been here a long long time, but the welcome is still old-fashioned and warm. Winter sports are enhanced by the thought of a sauna when you come back. Charlie and Marilyn Schubert are young, vigorous, attractive and fun. Charlie was in public relations and Marilyn was an airline stewardess, and if that doesn't give them a running start on being innkeepers, we don't know what does. The bar is a lively spot for the local residents as well as travellers.

The Schuberts have a lot of ski-touring equipment, and this new version of an old sport is one of the most popular winter sports available when you stay at Barrows House. You can leave from the front door!

The menu is lovely, and in summer the fresh vegetables are unusually prepared, Sauteed Cucumbers in Dill, Zucchini, Peppers and Onions, are some of them, and they change with what is fresh at the moment. Sissy Hicks presides over the kitchen and is also an avid gardener. Whatever the season, Barrows House is open all year, and how many inns turn down your bed at night? Too darn few.

E: This one is high on my preferred list and should be popular with golfers, as the Dorset Field Club extends golfing privileges to Inn guests.

S: Marilyn's garden grows more beautiful every year, and the fern garden is a refreshing corner of green coolth.

A well run inn and a man on a diet go together about as well as an arsonist and a bale of hay.

Dorset Inn
Dorset, Vermont
05251

Innkeeper: Fred G. Russell
Telephone: 802-867-5500
Rooms: 45, practically all with private bath, or connecting bath.
Rates: MAP $15, single; $30 double. EP $9 single; $16 double.
Facilities: Closed October to Christmas, April to early June. Breakfast, Lunch and Dinner. Bar. Parking. TV. Wheelchair accessibility to dining room.

HOW TO GET THERE:

Leave I91 at Brattleboro, take Route 100 north to Londonderry, then left on Route 30 to Dorset. Or take Route 7 to Manchester Center then north on Route 30.

This is the oldest inn in Vermont, and it has been continuously operated as an inn. There is nothing antique about the welcome you receive, however. The Dorset Field Club, sporting one of Vermont's oldest 9-hole golf courses, extends golf priviledges to guests of the Inn. Summer or winter, this is a fine place to stay. Fred Russell is running the Inn for his father-in-law, Fred O. Whittemore, and doing a good job. There are 🐾 Wednesday night cookouts and Sunday night buffets that everyone looks forward to.

If culture turns you on, the Southern Vermont Arts Center, and the Dorset Playhouse will provide the comedy or drama of the theater. In summer, swim in the beautiful pool at the Inn, go boating on Emerald Lake, or go horseback riding over old, forgotten roads, past old stone fences.

🐾 Some inns have dogs, and some have cats, but Dorset Inn has fish, beautiful black angels, swimming in large aquariums. There is also a beautiful collection of Cantonware on the chimney face.

There is all sorts of great skiing within easy driving distance of the Inn, and as many places, they feature "Ski weeks," and "Ski weekends" with late-arrival snacks, après-ski fondue, hot wine punch and popcorn.

> *If you have never been drawn shivering from the warmth of a good bed by the sizzling lure of bacon on the grill, you have never been in a country inn.*

Waybury Inn
East Middlebury, Vermont
05740

Innkeepers: Mr. and Mrs. Warren A. Greene (Bud and Betty)
Telephone: 802-388-4015
Rooms: 11, 8 with bath.
Rates: Double rooms, $13–$17. For families of 4, 2 bedrooms with connecting bath $22.
Facilities: Open all year. Closed on Tuesdays from September 1 to June 1. Breakfast, Lunch and Dinner served. Bar. TV. Parking.

HOW TO GET THERE:

The Inn is located 29 miles north of Rutland, Vermont, on Route 125, in East Middlebury, Vt.

Waybury Inn was built in 1810, as a stagecoach stop at the foot of the Green Mountains, near one of the major east-west passes through the mountains. Most of the colonial atmosphere has been retained, but there is modern comfort as well. Bud and Betty Greene have seven children, and all but one, who is married, help out at the Inn. All the help is local, as a matter of fact. Hand hewn beams, wide pine boards, friendly fireplaces are the background for what one departing guest called the ➤"best Martini in Vermont". Country pleasures abound, at all times of year, hiking, swimming, golf, skiing, fishing and hunting are nearby. If it's culture you want, Middlebury College is only 5 miles away.

For the relaxed and unambitious visitor, the Inn has a wide porch, and a comfortable living room, there to read, doze, or meditate. ➤This Inn is off the main road, so it is delightfully quiet.

E: I had a marvelous conversation with a parrot called Barney the other morning. I did most of the talking.

S: The tap room downstairs is a beautiful room, and there is a lovely private dining room with barnside panelling and a fireplace. It's new, but it looks as if it has always been there.

> *I often wonder if a war could start if the heads of con-*
> *fronting nations spent an evening at a proper tavern.*

Old Town Farm Lodge
Gassetts, Vermont
05144

Innkeepers: Joseph and Lorraine Epler
Telephone: 802-875-2346
Rooms: 9, with 5 baths.
Rates: $16 per person. MAP. 12 years and under ½ rate.
Facilities: Open all year. Breakfast and Dinner served. No
Bar. Bring your own. Parking.

HOW TO GET THERE:
Gassetts is 5 miles north of Chester Depot on Route
103.

If you like to ski and you have youngsters, throw everything in the car and head for the Old Town Farm Lodge. There are four young Eplers, and a small white poodle already in residence. Meals are served family style, with one main course, simple, hearty, country food. The Lodge is located ☛in the heart of eleven ski areas, and the Eplers can direct you to where the skiing is best. Nearby there is hunting, fishing, hiking, golf, swimming and riding. They have it all, without the swinging nightlife enjoyed by the singles crowd.

The Lodge is busiest during the foliage season, so be sure to reserve ahead if you are going leaf-peeping. The Eplers are busy all year, restoring, rebuilding, replacing the farm house which is over one hundred years old. It was once known as The Town Farm, because that is where the indigent of the neighborhood were given food and lodging in return for a hard day's work on the farm.

E: The handmade spiral staircase that curves to the second floor is so beautiful, and it has been painstakingly restored to its original condition.

S: The spick and span rooms are inviting, comfortable, and just right for the family.

"*The righteous minds of innkeepers
Induce them now and then,
To crack a bottle with a friend
Or treat unmoneyed men.*"
G. K. Chesterton

The Old Tavern
Grafton, Vermont
05146

Manager: Hunter Moss
Telephone: 802-843-2375
Rooms: 37, all with private bath.
Rates: EP, single $25–$45, double, $20–$40.
Facilities: Closed in April. Breakfast, Lunch and Dinner. Swimming. Tennis. Nature walks. TV in lounge. Bar. Parking. Elevator.

HOW TO GET THERE:

Exit 5 from I91, at Bellows Falls, to Route 121, which comes before you negotiate the entire exit ramp, so keep a sharp eye out.

Over the hills and far away is a Vermont village called Grafton. The Old Tavern there has been operated as an inn since 1801. Since 1966, when the inn was purchased by the Windham Foundation it has been restored so that it is one of the superb New England inns we all are seeking.

When you turn the car off the pounding interstate highway to the tree shaded route that winds to this quaint village you step back in time. The loveliest of the old combined with the comfort of the new makes an unbeatable inn. No grinding motors disturb your slumber in ✎ the best beds in all New England. The sheets and towels are the finest money can buy, there are extra pillows and blankets in each room. The spacious rooms are filled with antiques, all in mint condition.

There is no "organized activity" at the Old Tavern. ✎ The swimming pool is a natural pond, cool and refreshing. There are tennis courts nearby, and marked trails in the woods for walkers. This is the place to calm your spirits, recharge your batteries.

The cocktail barn is charming, connected to the Inn with a covered walk. There are flowers everywhere, hanging in baskets, in flower boxes, and on various tables in the gracious public rooms. The food here is excellent, unusual soups, varied entrees, cooked well, and served by pleasant waitresses.

E: The houses across the street that are also part of the Inn enchant me.

S: Carry me back to the Old Tavern! It is an ideal Inn, managed with heart.

Highland Lodge
Greensboro, Vermont
05841

Innkeepers: Carol and David Smith
Telephone: 802-533-2647
Rooms: 13 rooms, 8 with private baths, others share.
Rates: MAP single, $26, to $36; double $45 to $55, tax and tips included.
Facilities: Closed April 1 to May 30, and after the foliage until December 15. Breakfast and Dinner. Beer and wine license only, setups are available. Parking. Swimming and boating on Caspian Lake. Tennis.

HOW TO GET THERE:

Greensboro is 35 miles north east of Montpelier, Vermont. Take I91 as far as it goes. When it stops switch to Route 5 north to St. Johnsbury. Take Route 2 west out of town. At Danville take Route 15, turn right on Route 16, which will bring you into Greensboro. Go left out of town, and keep left. Caspian Lake is on your left, and the Inn is on the right side of the road.

Highland Lodge is really the place to get away from it all. With peace and quiet, delicious home cooked meals, and the delightful Smith family, you can recharge your batteries for life today. Don't mistake us, there is lots to do here in Greensboro. Caspian Lake, with the Lodge's own beach house is just across the road, with swimming, canoeing, sailing and fishing. Tennis, golf, and riding are available for those inclined.

People come back year after year to this friendly place. There are book-lined walls, puzzles to while away a long afternoon, but mostly a good mix of "genuine real down home kind of folks feeling" which comes over you as soon as you walk in. There is "recreation house" with supervised play for the youngsters, so this can be a real vacation for parents.

In the fall this is one of the great spots for foliage, and it isn't far to the White Mountains, or the Green Mountains, and cross country skiing in winter is a new found delight in this unspoiled country. This area is personally recommended by our publisher, who used to summer in Greensboro.

&: The giant geraniums turn me on.

S: I like to stroll to town. It isn't very big, when you get there, but there is a really good country store.

> *For one night at least let me escape from all those things the Puritans tell me I must face. Let me find a friendly inn.*

The Windridge Inn
Jeffersonville, Vermont
05464

Innkeeper: Alden Bryan
Telephone: 802-644-8281
Rooms: 5, all with bath.
Rates: Double, $22-$24 per person EP, December to May, European plan in summer.
Facilities: Open all year, except closed for lunch on Mondays. Breakfast in our bakery-dairy bar just next door. Lunch and Dinner at the Inn. Sunday dinner served 12:30-8. Bar. Parking. Tennis, indoor and out. Skiing.

HOW TO GET THERE:

Jeffersonville is northeast of Burlington, Route 15 from there will bring you right into Jeffersonville. Take Exit 10 from I89 at Waterbury, then take Route 100 north to Hyde Park. Turn left on Route 15.

Part of this little inn is as old as it looks, and it has that New England charm, all right, from the patchwork quilts on the comfortable twin beds, to the handmade braided rugs. The name of the game here is tennis, indoor, outdoor, clay courts, by day or night, with a heated lounge and dressing rooms. Of course, you're not all that far from Stowe, either. So the skiing is great, and the Inn has some good ski weeks offered, Sunday evening to Friday morning, except on holiday weeks.

What is really different and engaging about Windridge Inn is that Salle de Poulet. All across one side of the dining room is long narrow window. There is a slatted blind that pulls across this. When it is open you are gazing into the homelife of some Silver Sea Bright Bantam Chickens, and the cock really loves the limelight. They are really pretty, and fun to watch.

The luncheon menu is really inspired, Eggs Benedict, Salade Nicoise, Omelets, Chipped Beef in mushroom wine sauce, and they have Lowenbrau. The dinner menu is also very good, French kind of food, and the famous Windridge Breads, baked right there.

"There is nothing which has been contrived by man by which so much happiness is produced as by a good tavern or inn." Samuel Johnson

Rabbit Hill Inn
Lower Waterford, Vermont
05848

Innkeepers: Ruth and John Carroll
Telephone: 802-748-9766
Rooms: 20, all with bath.
Rates: $20–$28.
Facilities: Closed Christmas Eve and Christmas Day, Tuesdays in winter.

HOW TO GET THERE:

Take Route 2 from St. Johnsbury turn right to Route 18. Or from Route 5 take Route 135.

Rabbit Hill was reconstructed and modernized in 1956 with the belief that everyone in this mad world must have a place to retreat to, to rest, relax and recharge the batteries. The Inn wasn't always as peaceful as it is today, the old drovers and loggers made it their stamping ground.

The Carrolls have owned the inn for eight years, and hope to own it many more. They are collectors at heart, he has ▰chess sets, and she has a marvelous collection of ▰ Hummel figurines. The Inn is located on Pucker Street, White Village, Waterford, Vt. White Village is so-called because a man from St. Johnsbury bought all the houses on Pucker Street and painted them white with green shutters. There is a lovely old church, and a ▰library that operates without a librarian, you just go and sign out your book yourself.

There is an ice cold pond for swimming, miles of country walks, Briar Patch Country Store, that is a *real* store, where they have a stock of rolling pins for brides, and a post office.

Stay awhile at Rabbit Hill and let the rest of the world go by.

"Venite ad me ownes qui stomacho laboratoratis et ego restaurabo vos."

"Come to me all whose stomachs cry out in anguish and I shall restore you."

The Okemo Inn
Ludlow, Vermont
05149

Innkeeper: Rhinard and Toni Parry
Telephone: 802-228-2031
Rooms: 12 rooms, 11 with bath.
Rates: MAP: in winter, $22 per person during week, $24 weekends and holidays. Summer, $20 double EP; $16 per person, MAP.
Facilities: Closed from the end of ski season to June 1. Open rest of the year. Swimming pool. Sauna. Honeymoon suite. Brass beds. Fireplaces. Cross Country Skiing trails.

HOW TO GET THERE:
> Exit 6 north from I91, follow Route 103 to Ludlow. Located one mile from Okemo Mt. Public transportation: Vermont Transit Bus lines, Amtrak to Bellows Falls.

Two little brown dogs named Fred and Barney welcome you when you arrive at Okemo Inn. Fast on their heels come the Rhinard Parrys, a couple of hard working youngsters who have a dear little baby boy. Their house has been there since 1810, but there's nothing old-fashioned about the swimming pool, and   the spacious sauna is the very thing to take the ache away after the first day of skiing.

Meals are served family style, hearty homecooked meals that feature Roast Beef, Ham, Turkey, Chicken, and if that fare seems a little plain, how about a little Stroganoff just for variety?

The Inn is practically at the foot of Okemo Mountain, a fast growing popular place to ski.

The Inn has a liquor license, and there is a color TV in the lounge. This seems an ideal spot for a couple, or young family who love to ski.

E: The brass beds caught my fancy.

S: The collection of "necessary china" for bedroom use in time bygone that is displayed on the bookshelf in the second floor hall is a wonder.

A good country inn should have a dog.

Reluctant Panther Inn
Manchester Village, Vermont
05254

Innkeepers: Woody and Joan Cornell
Telephone: 802-362-2568
Rates: $22–$24 double.
Facilities: 7 rooms, each with private bath and telephone. Closed April and May, and after the end of the foliage until December 23. Dining room closed Tuesday. Bar. Television. There is a teeny-weeny elevator, and there are steps leading into the house. Breakfast for house guests, no lunch. No children. No pets.

HOW TO GET THERE:

As you approach the Village of Manchester from the south on Route 7, look to the left and you will see the Panther.

You might not want to live with the ⬛️fabulous decor you find within the mauve walls of the Reluctant Panther, but it is certainly fun to wake up in some of the wildly amusing and comfortable guest rooms. A frothy mixture of old and new is unique and attractive. It is imperative to reserve well in advance. It is too good to miss.

The kitchen has just been entirely redone, the better to serve the excellent food the Panther is noted for. Smoked salmon, tiny whole trout served with mayonnaise and caper sauce, Greek lemon soup, and a variety of exotic crepes are only some of the delights awaiting you here.

The Cornells have a definite flair for the unusual in interior design. The rooms are charming, different and exciting. There are three golf courses nearby, as well as tennis. Marvelous skiing in winter, and Manchester is a pleasant village. Since the Panther is not open for lunch, try The Buttery at The Jelly Mill.

E: Under the enormous hanging basket in the garden room is my favorite breakfast spot.

S: I'm in love with the mushroom wallpaper, to say nothing of the heliotrope bathtub. And all those furry rugs going half way up the wall are terrific.

Hark, which are common noises and which are the ghosts of long contented guests.

The Silver Skates
Marlboro, Vermont
05344

Innkeeper: Hans Imboden
Telephone: 802-254-2894
Rooms: 8, all with private bath.
Rates: $18 double, $14 single.
Facilities: Open all year. Dining room open Tuesday through
   Saturday for Dinner. Breakfast served to house guests
   only. Lunch during the Marlboro Festival Season,
   July and August, Liquor license, no bar. Parking.

HOW TO GET THERE:
Exit from I91 at Exit 2, at Brattleboro. Take Route 9
to Marlboro.

Here you have a Swiss innkeeper, running a place called the Silver Skates, all done up in Delft tiles, but it is just because he hasn't changed the name. This place isn't fancy, but it is comfortable, and the food is outstanding. ☛ Sweetbreads aren't easy to find in New York. Here they are done in wine caper sauce that is a poem.

This is the nearest inn to the Marlboro Music Festival, so reserve early if you are a music lover. There is good skiing in winter, and all the wonderful Vermont activities, antique hunting, foliage in Autumn, are close at hand. Since Marlboro is at the bottom of the Green Mountain State, it really doesn't take very long to get there.

E: There is a real Ratskeller here, and I wonder if Hans would whip me up a fondue the next time I stop here, when winter comes.

S: I like the little bay windows in the rooms, gives the rooms a different touch.

> *And now once more I shape my way*
> *Thro' rain or shine, thro' thick or thin,*
> *Secure to meet, at close of day*
> *With kind reception, at an inn.*
> William Shenstone, 1714–1763
> (written at an Inn at Henley)

The Vermont Inn

Mendon, Vermont

05701

Innkeeper: Shirley Peabody
Telephone: 802-773-9847
Rooms: 10, 2 central baths, 1 private.
Rates: Winter MAP $15–19 per person. Summer EP $10–15.
Facilities: The Inn is closed on Tuesday. Breakfast for house guests. No lunch. Dinner. Bar. Television. Parking. Tennis. Golf. Skiing.

HOW TO GET THERE:
5 miles east of Rutland on Route 4.

You may be greeted at the door of this friendly red
house by a large boxer dog called Ugly III. He is inclined
to be a bit of a roamer, but he is most gracious when he is
at home.

The Vermont Inn is well-known locally for its really fine
food. Where else can you get a whole suckling pig on a
week's notice, or any notice, for that matter?

☞ Shirley is one of the few people I know who remembers that little children deserve attention, and includes
child's portions on her menu. Bravo. You are likely to find
a very mixed group of people at the Inn . . . young profes-
sional people from Boston or New York, families complete
with young. "Anything," Shirley says, "from honeymooners
to retireds."

S: There are salad bars, and then there is the one at The
Vermont Inn. Everything, I swear, everything.

---

*The dog nuzzled my leg. The fire sent out a glow. The
drink was good. Only at an inn.*

Middlebury Inn
Middlebury, Vermont
05753

Innkeepers: David E. Beach and family
Telephone: 802-388-4961
Rooms: 75, 65 with private bath, 40 air conditioned.
Rates: Single, $14 to $32, Double, $20 to $32.
Facilities: Open all year. Breakfast, Lunch and Dinner
served, Bar. Elevator. Parking. TV. Skiing. Fireplaces.

HOW TO GET THERE:

Right up Route 7, and you'll run right into Middlebury, and the Inn is right in the middle of town.

There has been an inn standing in the same location as the Middlebury Inn since 1788. There have been some changes, due to fire and the inroads of time, but the original brick building was constructed in 1827. 100 years later, the Middlebury Hotel Company took over, a new heating plant was installed, and extensive repairs were made. The Inn has a good central location, and of course, anyone who has anything to do with Middlebury College knows about the Inn.

It is being managed now by David Beach and his family. There is a delightful veranda café, and a really large lobby. The dining room is beautiful, and the food that is served there is delicious. Upstairs the wide halls wander and dip, up one step and down three, wide enough halls for ladies in hoopskirts to maneuver.

E: I could stay forever, mooning over the jigsaw puzzles in the lobby.

S: Every night there are popovers for supper! Heaven and then some.

> *In the autumn, especially as one ages, a firelit tavern in an excellent inn cannot be bettered by the stateliest mansions in Christendom.*

The Four Columns Inn
Newfane, Vermont
05345

Innkeepers: Rene and Anne Chardain
Telephone: 802-365-7713
Rooms: 14, all with private bath, 8 air conditioned.
Rates: Double rooms with private bath or shower from $28
    to $40.
Facilities: Inn is closed in April and November and on
    Mondays. Bar. Breakfast for house guests. Dinner
    served 6–9. TV. Dining room accessible to wheelchair.
    Parking.

HOW TO GET THERE:

220 miles from New York. 100 miles from Boston.
Take Exit 2 from I91 at Brattleboro to Route 30 north.
The Inn is 100 yards off Route 30 in Newfane.

If the hearty goodness of New England cooking should be starting to pall, turn your wheels toward The Four Columns Inn in Newfane. There in an authentic New England village, in a lovely old house, you will find superb continental cuisine with a menu that will tease every palate. Trout "au bleu," plucked living from their own tank, Curry Indonesian Style, assorted hors d'oeuvres Parisienne, Fresh Salmon Bernaise, Rack of Lamb for two and many other delectable dishes are served.

Owned and operated by Rene Chardain and his dear French wife, Anne, the Inn is a chef's dream come true.

Many of the rooms were made from the old barn that is connected Vermont style to the house. Though the beams are rough, the freshness of the decor belies the house's age.

The wine list is excellent, as is to be expected, but it is possible to obtain good American wine by the glass.

There is great swimming nearby, also wonderful skiing in winter. Newfane is a beautiful old town and a few days spent here might not be the best thing for your figure if you are not exercising, but when sublime food is at hand, who cares about anything else?

There is no anonymity in a country inn.

R.E. Carlson

Old Newfane Inn
Newfane, Vermont
05345

Innkeepers: Eric and Gundy Weindl
Telephone: 802-365-4427
Rooms: 10, 8 with private bath, 2 adjoining.
Rates: $28–$40.
Facilities: The Inn is closed Monday. Closed April to mid-
    May and November 15 to December 15. Continental
    Breakfast included with room. Lunch only in summer,
    Dinner year round. Bar. Parking.

HOW TO GET THERE:
    Take Route 30 North from Brattleboro.

Old is the right word to describe the Old Newfane Inn, founded in 1787, carefully kept so that modern day travellers are cradled in comfort. It is nearly impossible to list the prizes won by the chef-owner, Eric Weindl, the food is outstandingly excellent. The rooms, few in number, are furnished with antiques, papered with quaint flowered wallpaper, and attention has been paid to things like comfortable chairs, and lights to read by.

The dining room, with its beamed ceiling, is one of the most attractive we have come upon in our travels. Eric and Gundy have been here for seven years, and have become famous for the marvelous food they provide. World travellers, famous chefs, food writers all make the trip up to Newfane, a gem of a town, with a well deserved reputation as a garden spot of gastronomy.

E: How can I lose weight writing a country inn guide?

S: Finding superb continental food in an authentic country inn is what I call bliss.

The groaning breakfast board of a good inn always makes it difficult to remember the word "diet."

Norwich Inn
Norwich, Vermont
05055

Innkeepers: Barbara A. and William J. Dibble
Telephone: 802-649-1143
Rooms: 27, all with baths, 7 air conditioned.
Rates: Double, $18-$25, Single, $14-$18. MAP on request.
Facilities: Open all year. Breakfast, Lunch and Dinner. Bar. Cable TV in all rooms. Parking. Swimming near by. Skiing. Canoeing. Golf near by.

HOW TO GET THERE:
Exit 13 from I91 5 miles north of I89.

Right on the sign for the Inn it says since 1797, and truly said, because travelers up the beautiful Connecticut River Valley have been finding a warm welcome at this grand old house ever since. Just a mile away from Dartmouth College, alumni, skiers, tourists, and commercial travelers find a special homelike atmosphere, "dignified, but fun" said Bill Dibble.

Barbara Dibble's touch is seen in the attractive guest rooms, comfortable and roomy, with little chrome or plastic to intrude a modern feeling.

You can come to Norwich by air, car, bus, or rail, a rarity, today. Given advance notice you will be met at train or plane. Reserve well ahead for football weekends, because there is a great ██ room downstairs in the Inn, where the thick stone foundations of this old place are revealed, and whether the group is drowning their sorrow or celebrating a victory, this is where the crowd is.

The food is very good. There is an excellent salad bar and don't miss the ██ homemade oatmeal bread.

E: There's a dear little Victorian Bar off the living room. The green velvet chairs are adorable.

S: The big bow window in the dining room pleases me, but I think I like best to eat on the ██ beautiful flower filled porch, which is even used in winter! You must see it in the snow!

> *When the stars are lost and rain seeps coldly upon the ground, how wonderful to find a lighted inn.*

The Weathersfield Lodge
Perkinsville, Vermont
05151

Innkeepers: Peter and Dottie Ireland, and their children, Arthur, Debbie, Charles, and Jenny.

Telephone: 802-263-5445

Rooms: 5, most with bath and working fireplace.

Rates: Single, $9–$16; double, $16–$22. Fireplace $2.50. During October rates are $2 more for singles, and $4 more for doubles.

Facilities: Open all year. Breakfast and Dinner. Bar.

HOW TO GET THERE:

Exit 7 from I91. Route 106 north through Springfield. Look for the swinging blue sign on your left just before Perkinsville. For public transportation: Amtrak to Bellows Falls; planes at Rutland, or Keene charter flights available to Springfield Airport, 1 mile away; the Inn will meet buses at Springfield.

When you turn up the bumpy road that leads to this nice old farmhouse, you feel that time has turned backward. There is excellent skiing, horseback riding, gliding, and antiquing near the Lodge. The Irelands believe their role is to provide a comfortable and relaxed base from which their guests may explore and savor all of central Vermont.

Dottie does the cooking and it is served in what was once the carriage shed, but is now an intimate dining room where each table can see the fire in the huge fieldstone fireplace. The logo of the lodge is the horn of plenty and Dottie's food and Peter's drinks are always ample; but both are most proud of the quality.

Peter has a gun collection which he willingly shows to interested guests. When Mt. Ascutney is dressed in her fall colors, there is a lovely view from this friendly family Inn.

When you have but one night to spend which inn to choose is as difficult as the choice you had years ago at the penny candy counter, and equally rewarding.

Johnny Seesaw's
Peru, Vermont
05152

Innkeepers: Larry and Anne Ward
Telephone: 802-824-5533
Rooms: 22, all with bath, plus ski bunk rooms for juniors.
Rates: MAP. Adults at Inn $20–$26 each; in cottages, $27–$29 each, daily. Juniors, (by age) $13–$18 each.
Facilities: Closed end of skiing to July 1, and end of foliage until Thanksgiving. Breakfast. Dinner. (Picnic lunches extra.) Liquor license. TV. Parking. Swimming. Tennis. Skiing. Hunting.

HOW TO GET THERE:
220 miles from New York, 150 from Boston. From US Route 7 take Route 30 right at Manchester Depot. The Inn is 10 miles east on Vermont Route 11. From I91, exit 6 to Route 103 to Chester. The Inn is 20 miles west on Vermont Route 11.

Johnny Seesaw's is a place where they really welcome children: there are two, aged 7 and 4, in residence. There is an early dinner hour for them, and genuinely nice girls to help them make fun. The food at the Inn is good: fine country food prepared with imagination, including home-baked bread and home-made soup.

The Inn has a unique character, mostly because of the guests who keep coming back. It is set 2,000 feet up right on Bromley Mountain. The 65'x25'-sized pool, marble rimmed, is a great summer gathering place, and the tennis court is always ready. There are six nearby golf courses, and riding is offered at the Ox Bow Ranch near Weston.

For the many skiers who come to Vermont, Bromley's 5 chairlifts and GLM Ski School are right next door; Stratton and Magic Mts., the Viking Ski Touring Center and Wild Wings X-C are but a few minutes away.

For fishermen and hunters, or those who wish to take up the sport, the Orvis Fly-Fishing and Wing Shooting Schools in nearby Manchester, have classes. The Sportsman Classes are held twice weekly, 3-day sessions thru October, and participants may stay at the Inn. The nearby towns boast many attractive and interesting shops.

Ɛ: The circular fireplace in the lounge really attracts me, to say nothing of the cushioned platform along one side of the room. Did he really say "Seducerie?"

S: I just love the whole easy feeling you get when you come in this friendly Inn.

Cats, birds, flowers, and dogs in companionate confusion are to be found where hospitality has bested the world of commerce.

Saxtons River Inn
Saxtons River, Vermont
05154

Innkeepers: Averill Campbell Larsen and The Campbell
    Family
Telephone: 802-869-2110
Rooms: 12, 6 with private bath, 6 with baths to share.
Rates: $16-$30.
Facilities: Open all year. Restaurant closed Tuesday.
    Breakfast for house guests. Lunch and Dinner. Bar.
    Parking.

HOW TO GET THERE:
Take either Exit 5 or 6 at Bellows Falls, from I-91.
Saxtons River is on Rte. 121, and the Inn is on Main
Street in the center of town.

Blessings on the Campbell Family, and especially on Averill who has put it all together, brought every one home from the four corners of the earth, working to renovate this turn of the century Inn, and revitalize the little village of Saxtons River. ➤ Cross the wide front porch, come in the front door, to the right is a little breakfast room, to the left the copper bar, and straight on through to the dining room. Tiffany chandeliers light the flower bedecked tables, and some of the freshest, most original food is carried out from the spick-and-span kitchen to please the most particular diner.

➤ The guest rooms are spectacular, handsomely decorated with a combination of old furniture, and crisp new fabrics. Every room has something comfortable to sit on, good lights so you can read in bed or in a chair without having to re-wire the inn. Your Innkeeper has travelled around the world and knows what is needed for creature comforts. She has slept in every one of her guest rooms, an acid test. She has her own aerie in the topmost tower, five stories above the world of Saxtons River.

The menu changes, of course, with what is fresh and good in season. If you really aren't hungry, you can have soup and salad and bread for a most nominal price, or just a large vegetable salad. If you are starving, begin with soup, or mushroom maison, rumaki or ratatouille, and go on to a main course of steak, Chicken Louise, Coquille St. Jacques, or something equally tempting. Save room for dessert, they are apallingly good.

E: I love to read in bed and this is a comfortable place to do it.

S: Put The Saxtons River Inn high on your list of places not to be missed. New and wonderful.

The Londonderry Inn
South Londonderry, Vermont
05155

Innkeepers: John and Norma Luinetti
Telephone: 802-824-5226
Rooms: 27, each with private bath.
Rates: Summer and Fall, MAP, $21–$28 per person.
Facilities: Closed from October 20, until snow time, after
skiing until June 20. Breakfast for house guests. No
lunch. BYOB. Parking. Putting green. Billiard Room.
Golf. Skiing. Swimming Pool. Shuffleboard. Badmin-
ton.

HOW TO GET THERE:

Take Exit 1 or 2 from I-91 at Brattleboro, take Route
30 North to Rawsonville, then Route 100 to South
Londonderry.

This must be the cleanest inn in all New England. From the sparkling white paint outside, to the lovely colonial interior, the whole place just shines. The Luinettis have been here since 1949, and the pride they take in their Inn is evident from the moment you drive up the steep hill and turn in the driveway.

The Inn is centrally located for the Big 3 ski areas, Bromley, Magic and Stratton. There are trails marked for cross-country skiing on the 250 acres that surround the Inn. In the summer the avid golfer will find 8 golf courses within half an hour's ride from South Londonderry.

We were happy to hear Spanish being spoken here, our hosts like to vacation in Mexico, which is a real change from a country inn in Vermont. They serve very good food, supervised by John, who used to work at the Waldorf-Astoria in New York. The country breakfast is outstanding.

E: This is one inn where I don't have to bring my own pillow. The beds are perfection, and the pillows are down filled.

The church bell is often the pleasant interruption of a good night's sleep at an inn.

Marton's Fundador Lodge

South Londonderry, Vermont

05155

Innkeepers: Mort and Beryl Marton
Telephone: 802-297-1700
Rooms: 16 with bath and 3 bunk rooms, each with bath.
Rates: MAP. Double per person $27.50-$29.50. Additional
  person $17. Single occupancy $35. Family rooms
  $25-$29.50 per person, $17-$17.50 each additional
  person. Bunk rooms $22 and $18 for people under 14.
  Special ski week packages. EP Rates also available.
Facilities: Bar. Dining Room. Heated Outdoor Pool. Croquet (specialty). Beryl Marton's Cooking School at
  the Lodge. Cross-country skiing on the property in
  winter. Within minutes: Tennis, horseback riding,
  hiking, antiques, Summer Theatre at Weston.

HOW TO GET THERE:

Take Exit 2—Brattleboro—off Interstate 91. Follow
Route 30 North to South Londonderry (Rawsonville).
The Inn is on your left just beyond where Route 100
turns North.

There is no end to the things you can do right at this Inn and close by. For skiers you are but five minutes from Stratton Mountain. But skier or not, and winter or summer, Mort, in his quiet way, makes sure all the guests are happy. In ski season he gives a breakfast report on the snow conditions from every nearby slope and even cuts a wedge of snow, brings it in and proves to all how the skiing will be. Those left behind are offered trips to close-by areas for education and mostly for fun.

Beryl Marton is the chef and author of *The Complete Book of Salads* and *Diet for One, Dinner for All*, winner of the Tastemaker Award for the Best Cookbook in the field of Diet and Health Books. Needless to say the food here is superb. Reservations are a must. ⟡ Summertime the vegetables are fresh from their garden and wintertime fresh from California.

The main lounge room has a circular fireplace, a grand piano (for all to play), great couches, and card tables. ⟡ They also have a great library with books, books, books.

To complete this rather new Inn with older feelings is an intimate cocktail lounge where in winter and summer, Beryl serves an array of great and different hors d'oeuvres.

E: The movies Mort puts on from time to time are great shows.

S: I love the stone patio for lunch in Summer. It overlooks the lawn and pool.

> *The aroma of freshly baking bread told me surely I was awakening in a good country inn.*

Kedron Valley Inn
South Woodstock, Vermont
05071

Innkeepers: Paul and Barbara Kendall
Telephone: 802-457-1473
Rooms: 34, 31 with bath.
Rates: MAP: Single, $18.25-$32; Double, $16-$23 per person.
EP: Single, $6.25-$23; Double, $7-$14 per person.
Facilities: Closed in April. Breakfast, Lunch and Dinner.
Bar. TV in lounge, also some rooms. Some rooms
accessible to wheelchairs. Parking. Horseback riding
from own stables. Swimming in acre plus pond. Tennis.
Golf. Photography. Skiing. Skating.

HOW TO GET THERE:

Take Exit 8 from I91, take Rte 131 to Rte 106, turn
right and stay on 106 to South Woodstock. Take Exit 1
from I89, take Rte 4 into Woodstock, turn left on Rte
106 to South Woodstock.

At last, a Vermont country inn run by Vermonters! We thought we might not find one. Paul and Barbara Kendall are parents of 7th generation Kendalls, descendants of the pioneers who settled this lovely valley. The Inn itself dates from 1828, a lovely old building with a beautiful staircase.

There is so much to do in South Woodstock! The Green Mountain Horse Association is located here, an organization dedicated to the pleasures of horse breeding and riding. ☛ There are numerous marked trails through the woods, and beginners are welcomed as well as experts. You may even bring your own horse! John Doscher's School of Photography is located here, and the Inn has a duo-projector and screen which guests are free to use. There is an 18-hole golf course at the Woodstock Country Club, and guests may use it. Woodstock is just minutes away with its fine museum, Recreation Center with swimming pool and bowling alleys. Stay right at Kedron Valley and swim in summer in their ☛ lovely pond, and skate in winter; they even have lights around it for evening activity. And we have not even mentioned the seven different ski areas close to the Inn. The Inn will rent ski-touring equipment, and have three accomplished skiers on the staff to help the neophytes.

We haven't even mentioned the food and drink at the Inn. The bar is located next door in its own brick building. Long ago it was connected with a "floating dance floor" over the buggy shed, but this has disappeared.

ε: My favorite room is the one with the Paisley wallpaper and of course, a canopy bed!

S: The beautiful fireplaces in the Inn especially the two in the bedrooms are what I remember with affection.

The Hartness House
Springfield, Vermont
05156

Innkeeper: Ruth M. Crawford
Telephone: 802-885-2115
Rooms: 46 all with bath, phone, T.V., and air conditioned.
Rates: $12 to $26.
Facilities: Open all year. Breakfast, Lunch and Dinner served. Bar. Parking. Swimming. Bedboards. Some rooms available for wheelchairs, with ramped entrance. TV, some color. Golf nearby.

HOW TO GET THERE:

Springfield is 3 miles north of Exit 7 on I91, on Route 11 and 106. From the police booth in downtown Springfield go up Summer Hill starting right at the light. Keep going up the hill as it curves around and to the left until it levels off (cemetery on your right). At the 5-street intersection bear left on Orchard Street. 300 yards ahead of you you will find the Inn.

The history of this house and that of James Hartness who built it is fascinating, and too long to go into here. Go up to Springfield and stay awhile, and you will find out all the details. It is a lovely country inn, the house is a mansion built in 1904. Those Edwardian years were great for the building of some lovely American houses. James Hartness was a machine tool genius, astronomer, pioneer aviator, and Governor of Vermont. He was a recluse, and needed absolute quiet. He was married to a lovely butterfly of a lady, and this gracious house reflects both their tastes.

There is a magnificent stairway in the spacious hall. The dining room is a handsome room, presided over by two large portraits, one of Governor Hartness, one of his lady. There are twelve delightful rooms in the old Inn and a modern addition to the Inn contains 34 rooms. There is a clay tennis court and a serene swimming pool.

&: The underground tunnel, leading to the bar, and also to the Observatory with its telescope intrigues me.

S: Reserve the round room in the tower for me, I feel my Princess mood coming on.

> *A night at an inn adds a tinge to the coming day that cannot be described, only enjoyed.*

The Lodge at Smuggler's Notch
Stowe, Vermont
05672

Innkeeper: Mr. Gerhard Schmidt
Telephone: 802-253-7311
Rooms: 69, all with private bath or connecting.
Rates: MAP, $28 to $44 per person, several golf and ski plans.
Facilities: Closed Oct. 15–Dec. 15, April 15–June 15. Breakfast, Lunch (only in summer) and Dinner. TV. 2 fireplaces in suites, one in lounge. Game room. Parking. Heated pool. Music at meal time.

HOW TO GET THERE:

Amtrak goes to Waterbury, taxi from there. Greyhound goes to Burlington or Waterbury. Route 100 goes to Stowe. Regular plane flights to Burlington and Montpelier, car rentals at airport, bus or taxi to Stowe. Private and charter flights to Morrisville-Stowe airport.

This is an elegant, lovely inn, where everything is kept in mint condition, floors shining, windows crystal clear, flowers all over, so pack your best wardrobe pour le sport, and your prettiest long dress to wear into dinner.

The location, at Mt. Mansfield, up the hill through Smuggler's Notch, is fantastic. It is Alpine, to say the very least. The view is magnificent, and every window seems placed to catch it. All the help seem to smile all the time, how refreshing.

There is a wonderful game room, all the corridors leading to the rooms have flowers on the ceilings. The rooms are well furnished and comfortable.

In 1923 a farmhouse was converted into an inn, a really rustic summer resort, and over the years it has growed, like Topsy, and is now one of the most gracious inns in New England, and welcomes famous guests from all over the world.

E: The food is fabulous. The French chef has been at the Inn for more than 20 years, and the pastry chef makes such delicious goodies that I fear my ski pants will not fit!

S: Always creature comforts with me, I *do* love having my bed turned down for me at night.

> *The world grows smaller but fortunately we can always find another hidden corner for a good country inn.*

Echo Lake Inn
Tyson, Vermont
05149

Innkeeper: Dennis Scully
Telephone: 802-228-8602
Rooms: 19, Most rooms with connecting baths, a few with private, some close by.
Rates: $25 with private bath, $5 for additional person in room. Dormitory available, $8 per person.
Facilities: Open all year. Breakfast, Lunch and Dinner. Bar. TV in lounge. Heated swimming pool. Tennis. Golf. Fishing. Skiing. Boating and horseback riding.

HOW TO GET THERE:

Exit 6 from I91. Turn right on Route 100 in Ludlow, and you will find the Echo Lake Inn, in Tyson, before you get to Plymouth Union. Mail address: P.O. Box 142, Ludlow, Vt.

There's a tall personable Irishman keeping the Inn at Tyson. He wasn't always an innkeeper, but you'd never guess it. Dennis Scully calls himself a "big business dropout." This delightful old colonial inn has been welcoming travelers and vacationers for over 150 years. The guest rooms have been brightened with crisp new papers that reflect Mrs. Scully's good taste.

There's a cheery fire in the big lounge on winter days, and you can see the old spinning wheel, and learn how "Pop Goes the Weasel" came into being. ➤ The old colonial tavern is filled with old pictures, each with a tale to tell. In summer, the Inn has its own beach on beautiful Echo Lake, stream and spring fed, for swimming, boating and fishing (licenses are issued at the Inn). Hiking trails, horseback trails, hunting trails are all nearby.

There is a wealth of history in this old inn, many dignitaries have been guests here in the past, President and Mrs. McKinley, President Coolidge, Andrew Mellon, and many others. Tyson hasn't always been the sleepy crossroads you find today. During the Civil War, Tyson Furnace mined and smelted ore and manufactured the Tyson Stove. The old Cheese Factory next door to the Inn has been transformed into an antique shop, run by Mrs. Scully and the chef.

The lounge bar downstairs is a delight. The outside walls are natural Vermont stone. The fireplace in the center of the room is natural stone with great lounge chairs around it. There is a large bar and tables for your comfort.

E: The posters and pictures of gymnasts in the bar reflect the interest in the sport. Two of the Scully youngsters are gymnasts.

S: The fish are biting, and when you catch them, they can be frozen for you to take home at vacation's end.

Alexandre Georges

The Inn at Sawmill Farm
West Dover, Vermont
05356

Innkeepers: Rodney and Ione Williams
Telephone: 802-464-8131
Rooms: 14, with private bath. 2 that share a bath.
Rates: MAP $35 per person, 2 people in a room. $40 per person Deluxe rooms; $45 per person Suites with fireplaces.
Facilities: Open 7 days for Breakfast and Dinner. Bar. Parking. Swimming pool. Meditation deck. Tennis court. 2½ acre pond with trout fishing for guests. No credit cards. 15% gratuity added to your bill. Closed November 15–December 5.

HOW TO GET THERE:
Exit 2 on I91 at Brattleboro, to Route 9, at Wilmington turn right onto Route 100, into West Dover.

The Inn at Sawmill Farm was an old Vermont barn that Rod and Ione Williams have transformed into the gayest, warmest, most attractive place to stay we have seen in many a long mile. The bright colors used throughout the Inn reflect Ione's training as an interior designer, and the creative use of old wood and modifications to the Inn and two other houses, reflect Rod's training as an architect. All done in such fine taste. The rooms are very different. Some are sort of Victorian in feeling, and ➤ the ones that have little lofts for sleeping children are just great, you know, privacy, without being separated from them. Some of the suites have their own fireplaces. All are color coordinated with thick towels and extra pillows. ➤ We had fresh fruit in our suite, really great after a long trip to bite into a crisp harvest apple.

The kitchen is run by the Williams's son and his food is superb. Breakfast is on the patio which is decorated with beautiful hanging plants and overlooks the pool. ➤ Fresh orange juice and fresh fruits are served in iced bowls.

The Pot Belly Lounge is the bar, or if you prefer you can sit in the lounge room with a tremendous fireplace and look out into the treetops. There's a Golden Labrador retriever named Ginger who helps run the Inn. We could rave on for hours. Wherever you go, it is great.

E: The copper collection around the fireplace is so unusual. And the huge copper topped coffee table nearby is a beauty.

S: I'm torn between two favorite things, the lovely little library in the hayloft over the living room for the solitary reader, and the *shingled* walls in some of the bathrooms. Oh, yes, there's another . . . the meditation deck that is slightly removed from the pool area, for other solitary souls.

Windham Hill Farm
West Townshend, Vermont
05359

Innkeepers: The Folsom Family
Telephone: 802-874-5951
Rooms: 11, some with private baths, capacity 26 with bunk rooms for youngsters or skiers.
Rates: MAP, $18-$22, weekly rates, deposit required.
Facilities: Closed after foliage until snow falls. Closes around the end of snow, opens around June 1. Breakfast and Dinner. No bar. Bring your own. Complimentary wine served with dinner.

HOW TO GET THERE:

North from Greenfield on I91, take 2nd Brattleboro exit (marked W. Brattleboro and Vt. 9); then east on Vt. 9 to Brattleboro main street; North 3 blocks to Exxon Station, bear left on Vt. Route 30 to West Townshend (21 miles). At "Country Store" (closed), turn right up hill (Windham Road). 1½ miles to Windham Hill Farm sign on right.

At Windham Hill Farm you are sitting on the top of the world looking down on creation. The West River Valley stretches as far as the eye can see. Except for a small farmhouse on a neighboring hilltop there is no sign of man's unkindly hand. This 135-year-old farmhouse, lived in by one family until it was bought by the Folsoms, has been carefully restored.

Meals here are memorable. Hugh Folsom's mother (who occasionally inhabits the neighboring barn with her retired husband) studied cooking at the Cordon Bleu and has passed on her expertise to her son. Young Mrs. Folsom takes time from supervising the rearing of three youngsters to do all the baking, making mousses, cakes and souffles. In season all the vegetables are fresh, many of them grown right on the farm. There is a fresh water pond used for swimming in summer, skating in winter, and a new terrace building that overlooks it. Indoors there are books, music, piano, games, television, old magazines, fireplaces, library and lounge. No bar as such, but complimentary wine is served with dinner, and you are welcome to bring your own cocktails.

If you are looking for one of the more remote, exquisite, peaceful, and captivating places to unwind, forget your cares and utterly relax in an unorganized way, come to Windham Hill Farm.

&: Persuade Mrs. Folsom Sr. to show you her jade plant, and her private view of the Valley from the Barn Terrace.

S: I am waiting for it to rain so I can spend the whole day poking about in the barn. You will understand why when you see it.

The Inn at Weston
Weston, Vermont
05161

Innkeepers: Stu and Sue Douglas
Telephone: 802-824-5804
Rooms: 13, 10 with baths.
Rates: Summer: bed and breakfast $20–$24. Winter: MAP, $20–$24 per person.
Facilities: Breakfast, Lunch (weekends only) and Dinner. Lunch not served in winter. Sunday Brunch. Closed November and mid-April to mid-May. Dining room closed Tuesday. Open for rooms always. Bar. TV. Fireplace in lounge.

HOW TO GET THERE:
Off Route 91, exit 6, Route 103 to Chester. Take Route 11 to Londonderry, turn right on Route 100 to Weston. The Inn is in the Village.

If you walk in the front door of this lovely Inn, you are in Sue Douglases kitchen and Sue is the chef. She greets you with a warm smile and great culinary treats. The weekend we were there, the fare was ➤ Poached Salmon with mustard sauce, Roast Beef, Chicken Kiev and a Greek dinner salad. There is a different dinner salad served each night.

Keeping it all in the family, Stu Douglas is the bar-keeper and wow he makes a good martini. His domain has a ➤ small bar (a two seater) a fireplace, assorted cheeses and at regular intervals, or as Sue puts it, "as required," Jack Straw plays the piano and sings.

The rooms are small, very very pleasant with old antique beds that are comfortable. The dining room has so much charm and warmth, the walls are real barn siding, and everyone who works here ➤ smiles. They are a happy group.

Weston is the home of the Vermont Country Store. It is a short stroll down the road, and a mecca for browsers. The Inn is close to several ski areas, so do come and enjoy —as the Douglases say, "This is where friendships begin," and they really do.

E: Stu is the breakfast chef and makes among other things great whole-wheat pancakes.

S: The wooden toy maker down the road is great for grandmothers.

New England Inn
Woodstock, Vermont
05091

Innkeepers: Skip and Beth Pile
Telephone: 802-457-9804
Rooms: 9, 3 with private bath, others share.
Rates: $14–$18.
Facilities: The Inn is open 7 days a week, except for 2 weeks in November and 2 weeks in April. Skiing. Golf. Riding.

HOW TO GET THERE:
The Inn is located on Route 4 East, in Woodstock.

We admire an inn that serves breakfast to all comers. And such good breakfast. The red checkered tablecloths on the summer porch brighten up the day. This is an old house that had really fallen on evil days. ☛ The Piles have come along and are painstakingly restoring it. There are hanging baskets all over, plants in a sunny window on the stair landing, just everywhere you look. Beth not only has green fingers, she is really knowledgeable about food, and has made some memorable menus. She and Skip take turns at the Inn, so one of them is always there. When things get busy they sometimes pass each other in the hall, or don't really get to talk, except on the phone, for days.

S: My favorite room is the one in front with the flower strewn veranda.

E: They can send a Gladys Cooper up to the veranda any time. A fantastic, delicious rose colored drink that slips right down.

I have enjoyed the hospitality of a good inn and I am ready for the day ahead.

Canaan Inn
Canaan, New Hampshire
03741

Innkeeper: Laurie Blizzard
Telephone: 603-523-4846
Rooms: 28, 11 baths.
Rates: Rooms from $7.50 to $20.00. Based on double oc-
cupancy: MAP, $20 a day per person.
Facilities: Inn closed in April. Dining room closed on Mon-
day. Breakfast, Lunch and Dinner. Bar. Television.
Live entertainment on weekends. Closed 3 weeks in
April.

HOW TO GET THERE:
Where Route 4 meets Route 118, only a short way
from major highways. Exit 17 from I93, or get off
I91 to Route 89E. At exit 17, take Route 4, 13 miles east
to Junction 118. 5½ hours from New York, 3½ hours
from Hartford, 2 hours from Boston.

At last, an inn where you can take your horse. The Innkeeper can arrange to have you stable your horse at the old fair grounds. You can travel for miles, all day, in fact, ➤ on beautiful mountain trails. Laurie Blizzard has been working for five years, restoring this old hotel. The town of Canaan had a disastrous fire about fifty years ago. The Inn was saved, and served as a church and town hall for many years. The Mansard roof, the wrap-around veranda, and the winding staircase in the lobby all point to the Victorian birthday in 1876 of this marvelous old relic.

The food here is excellent, with an accent Italiano. Three meals a day are served, beginning with a country breakfast, a sandwich lunch or a salad bowl if you are so inclined, and a delightful dinner menu that features Duckling a l'Apricotte, Steaks, Veal a la Marsala, and a Honey Spiced Barbecue Chicken.

The Inn is open all year except for three weeks in April. There are snow activities, cross-country skiing, as well as swimming and hiking in the summer. Cardigan Mountain School, an excellent preparatory school for boys is close by, and the Canaan Inn is a haven for visiting parents.

E: The Tiffany style lamps in the lounge that light the pool table (billiards?) please me.

S: Try a hot oven grinder for lunch. It is outstanding. Or an omelet, or a large salad. The Inn's special cheese cake makes you come back for more.

Stafford's in the Field
Chocorua, New Hampshire
03817

Innkeepers: Ramona and Fred Stafford
Telephone: 603-323-7766
Rooms: 8, 2 with private baths, others share. Cottages.
Rates: MAP, $52–$58 double.
Facilities: Open May 30 thru Nov. 1 and Christmas thru
   April 1: telephone and check. Breakfast and Dinner
   served. No bar, but setups are available. No television.
   Parking. Meals only for Inn guests.

HOW TO GET THERE:

Take I93 north from Concord, take Route 104 to
Meredith, then Route 25 to Whittier, then Route 113
to Chocorua. Before you get into Chocorua look along
the left, and you will find a little road that will bring
you to Stafford's. Coming south from Conway take
Route 16, and turn right in Chocorua. The Inn road
will be on your right.

Stafford's in the Field is an impossible collection of contradictory things that adds up to an enchanting place to bring your tired mind, body and jaded palate, and get fixed up good as new. Eleven years ago the Stafford's transplanted themselves from California to this wonderful old farm, (part of the house is almost 200 years old) settled in with the children, and they are still working to make it the most engaging and different place on the eastern seaboard (in the woods.) Where to begin? ➤ The barn. On summer nights, Sundays, there is a string quartet. The barn's acoustics are remarkable. Thursday nights there is square dancing. The children are still there, growing up. The daughter of the house is responsible for the really sinful desserts.

Ramona Stafford likes to cook, a sort of French country thing, with wine and spices and herbs, fresh vegetables, only for guests, nobody from outside, and if she thinks it would go well, she even throws a ➤ little Mexican, really Mexican, dinner. Breakfasts are scrumptious, Eggs Benedict, or waffles on Sunday. Omelettes, most every day, but what a choice! Sour cream and green chiles, mild country cheddar, or cheddar and salsa, or eggs any style, from Ramona's own chickens.

Fred Stafford says there is an inexhaustible supply of ➤ "nature things to do." Just sitting watching the swallows swoop, or a leaf spin slowly to the ground restores what you've lost in today's busy world. Look at a mountain, play croquet, breathe that unpolluted air.

Turn in the lane some snowy evening, and see Stafford's glowing in the field, waiting to welcome you to a world well lost. They feature cross country skiing on their own trails.

ε: Bulah, a Brittany Spaniel, and Thomas the cat, are the chief animals in residence. Heart-warming to see the wagging tail and hear the purr in welcome.

S: Along with everything else, you know the food is outstanding and I'd come back any day for just one more bite that Ramona cooked.

Fitzwilliam Inn
Fitzwilliam, New Hampshire
03447

Innkeepers: Charles and Barbara Wallace
Telephone: 603-585-9000
Rooms: 23 rooms, 14 baths
Rates: EP, MAP and AP, from $8 per person, EP to $15; MAP from $17.50 to $24.50, AP from $20.50 to $27.50. Send for rates sheet.
Facilities: Open every day of the year. Breakfast, Lunch and Dinner served. Bar. TV. Swimming pool. Sauna. Skiing.

HOW TO GET THERE:
205 miles from New York, 65 miles from Boston. On Routes 12 and 119. Vermont Transit bus stops at the Inn.

"The more plastic motels that are built, the more people are going to be driven back to a warm country inn without wall-to-wall carpeting, but with something else." Enoch Fuller said this. And the Fitzwilliam Inn which he owned and ran until his death a few years ago is indeed a warm country inn. The Fitzwilliam Inn is still the old-fashioned New England inn that has been offering food, grog and lodging to weary travelers since 1796.

If sleigh riding is your idea of a great winter sport, book yourself in at Fitzwilliam. ☛ In summer there is square dancing in the village. There are 12 antique shops in this little town. The bar is a great little tap room, where hot winter drinks are called "Broken Legs." The meals are hearty New England affairs, with a wonderful homemade ☛ Pumpkin bread, and homemade desserts. The menus are tacked to little bread boards.

The Wallace's like to have music at the Inn, concerts every Sunday in the winter, and on special occasions. In summer you can enjoy the beautiful pool, after ☛ the sauna, then lunch on the patio beside the pool. All this, with the charm of a centuries old inn, lovely antiques, and a cordial welcome from the innkeeper.

E: The glowing fire in the taproom warmed The Icy Travellers, taking refuge from an April snowstorm.

S: The fringed muslin curtains in the parlor are a delight, with the Victorian furniture and the old square piano.

> *A cricket on the hearth of a country inn is music beyond the angels.*

Sugar Hill Inn
Sugar Hill, Franconia, New Hampshire
03580

Innkeepers: Estelle and Bernard Gould
Telephone: 603-823-5621
Rooms: 9, 7 with private baths.
Rates: EP from $18 to $26 per person. AP on request.
Facilities: Closed November till mid-December. Pub Lounge.
TV. Addition suitable for wheelchairs. Parking.
Heated pool. Golf. Skiing. Fishing. Hunting.

HOW TO GET THERE:
Halfway up Sugar Hill from Franconia, N.H. on Route
117, take Exit 38 from I93 into Franconia.

Once you get to Sugar Hill you won't want to leave, so plan to stay for a few days. If pollution has you down, come up the hill for a delightful change. The Pewter Pub is a most attractive little bar and the Bloody Marys are excellent.

The food is all homecooked, soups from scratch, fresh baked bread, special house salad dressing. Apple Pandowdy for dessert or homemade pie finish off a delightful meal. The "new chef" is Lilymae Richardson, who is well-known locally as the owner and founder of the Richardson's Creamery. Lilymae specializes in down to earth rib roast of beef, roast loin of pork and Indian pudding. For the diner with a more sophisticated taste, there is baked cornish hen, beef ragout, or seafood Newburg.

This Inn was formerly called the Caramat, and has been an inn since 1925. The house itself dates from 1750, an old farmhouse that has been converted to modern use. The inn dog is Gentle Norman. There is a nice relaxed feeling about the place. The pool in summer is refreshing and there are many wooded trails for walking.

S: I like the hand-sewn appliques of mountain scenes created by local artists.

If all inns were alike they simply would not be inn.

163

The John Hancock Inn
Hancock, New Hampshire
03449

Innkeepers: Glynn and Pat Wells
Telephone: 603-525-3318
Rooms: 10, all with bath.
Rates: $15 single, $20 double.
Facilities: Open all year, except one week early spring and
     fall. Breakfast, Lunch and Dinner served. Lounge.
     Parking. Swimming at pond. Bicycles loaned.

HOW TO GET THERE:

> From Boston take Route 128, then Route 3 to 101 West.
> Hancock is located just off Route 202 above Peter-
> borough.

Operated as an inn since 1789, the John Hancock has new, young owners, the Wells family. Carefully preserved is The Mural Room, believed to date back to the early years of the Inn. The Carriage Lounge is very unusual, tables made from giant bellows from an old foundry in Nova Scotia, and the seats are made from old buggy seats. The name stems from the fact that John Hancock, the founding father one, once owned most of the land that is the present town of Hancock. Set among twisty hills with a weathered clapboard facade, graceful white pillars and a warm red door, the Inn represents all that is good about old inns. Warm welcomes, good food, sound drinks, and good beds, set in a quiet town that hasn't changed much in the last two centuries.

Dinner is served by candlelight, and when the winter storms howl through the hills the fireplace in the bar has a crackling fire to warm your heart and your toes. Braided rugs cover part of the wide board floors, and primitive paintings hang on the walls.

Swim in summer in Norway Lake, within walking distance of the Inn. Climb mountains, or just sit and listen to the church chimes during foliage time. Alpine and cross-country skiing nearby in winter. Browse in the antique shops on a cool spring morn.

I love all good inns, but secretly I have a rather special fondness if the boniface is fat.

Colby Hill Inn
Henniker, New Hampshire
03242

Innkeepers: The Glover Family
Telephone: 603-428-3281
Rooms: 8, 4 with private bath, 4 that share.
Rates: $10-$12 single, $14-$16 double.
Facilities: Open all year, closed Mondays, Breakfast and
    Dinner. Sunday dinner starts at noon. Liquor license
    for meal service. TV. Parking. Swimming.

HOW TO GET THERE:

Go up I91 to Brattleboro. Take Route 9 east into
Henniker.

This picturesque old house dates back to 1800, it leans and dips a bit here and there, but that only adds to the charm. The wide floor boards are authentic, you can't buy them like that nowadays. Don Glover Jr. is Chief Innkeeper, he supervises the cooking and everything else that needs doing in a country inn. His parents came up from New Jersey to lend a hand, and he has a young wife and small son. There is a young black dog named Tar, what else, who nearly loses his tail with each welcome.

The meals are simple and delicious. Steak or Chicken served in different ways, lots of fresh seafood, including salmon, and a dessert list that would tempt a saint, English Lemon Curd and Chocolate Mousse among the items. The next door neighbors have a garden and supply fresh vegetables in season. Henniker is a little college town, and if you happen to have a youngster there, it is grand to have such a nice place to stay.

"Does the road wind uphill all the way?
  Yes, to the very end.
Will the day's journey take the whole day long?
  From morn to night, my friend."
                                        Christina Rossetti

Dick Smith

The New England Inn
Intervale, North Conway, New Hampshire
03845

Innkeepers: Gail and Bill Paine
Telephone: 603-356-5541
Rooms: 40, all with bath. Cottages with fireplaces.
Rates: MAP, $22 to $40.
Facilities: Closed at the end of foliage, until mid-December, and mid-April to June. Breakfast, Lunch and Dinner served. Bar. Accessible for wheelchairs. Parking. Swimming pool, Hiking Trails, Ski Touring. Golf (4 holes). Tennis. 3 clay courts. Piano Bar. Dancing on Friday and Saturday night.

HOW TO GET THERE:

North Conway is close to the Maine border, at the Gateway to the White Mountains, on Route 302.

Intervale, North Conway

This is a complete Inn, that just grew and grew. It started as a farm in 1883, and now has cottages, and tennis courts, and a swimming pool, and a lovely dining room and a beautiful bar, but it still has the same old comfortable feeling that brings guests back year after year. You can still stay in the old house, and the parlor has a table with a cribbage counter carved right in it.

The staff is friendly, the chef has been here 29 years, his wife is the dining room hostess. The innkeeper is young in years, but long in experience. The bartender is friendly, and he knows when to offer two weary ladies a cool drink in his air conditioned bar when New Hampshire's weather turns strangely warm. Hot tea and cocoa are welcome when the skiers return from the slopes on wintery days. The Ravine Room, with its fabulous painting of Tuckerman's Ravine by David Baker is a gathering spot all year round. Saturday nights there is dancing, and the Piano Bar adds to the conviviality.

The food is really excellent, North Country Breakfasts with Porridge and Home Fried Potatoes, Fresh Doughnuts and Hot Muffins are outstanding. Steak and Lobster shine on the dinner menu, along with Prime Ribs and Baked Sugar Cured Ham with Raisin Sauce. The desserts are divine, Fresh Strawberry Shortcake, and even a Grand Marnier Parfait.

E: I love this place, winter, spring, summer and fall.

Come back 100 years and stay at my inn.

Christmas Farm Inn
Jackson, New Hampshire
03846

Innkeepers: The Powers Family
Telephone: 603-383-4313
Rooms: 25, 23 with private bath.
Rates: MAP, from $16 per person to $22. Children's rates.
  Rooms in Main House, A 1771 salt box and a log
  cabin, as well as the Sugar House, a 2 room suite, and
  bunk rooms for up to 6 people.
Facilities: Closed November and May. Breakfast, Lunch
  (picnics packed) and Dinner served. No bar, but a
  dining room license. TV. Parking. Very scenic. Skiing.
  Swimming. Summer theater at Eastern Slopes Inn,
  nearby. Putting green.

HOW TO GET THERE:

By Trailways bus to Jackson from Boston. Inn will
meet bus. By car: Go north from Portsmouth on the
Spalding Turnpike (Route 16) all the way to the covered
bridge at Jackson. Turn right over bridge and follow
16B through Jackson Village and up the hill. The Inn
is ¼ mile beyond the village. Two hours drive from
Portsmouth.

Christmas Farm is a present to everybody, a lovely old farm house and its outbuildings made into an inspired country inn. The Powers Family have owned the Inn for the last 3 years, and with the two boys, Wayne and Glenn, the St. Bernard named Holly, some sheep that Wayne is raising as his 4-H project, have really made this a homelike place. Come with your baby, they'll warm the bottles, find a babysitter; come with your grandmother, there's a rocking chair for her if she isn't out on the slopes, grandmothers being what they are these days.

With 25 rooms the Inn is big enough to give good service, but not so large that guests are lost in the crowd. The Powers enjoy knowing their guests.

The food is excellent, three times a day, simple, but well-prepared. Swedish bread is featured, and there is a nice wine list.

The views from the Inn are spectacular, and there is a lovely pool just across the road from the Main House, just far enough away so that happy swimmers won't disturb your afternoon nap.

Come in the fall for the glorious foliage, or ski at any of 5 major areas from one to eight miles from the Inn. You are absolutely surrounded by the White Mountains here in Jackson.

E: I truly love Christmas, so Christmas Farm is automatically one of my favorite places.

S: Summertime gal that I am, I love an inn that will mix up a light and icy Sangria. Served right on the porch, too, so I can enjoy the garden.

Dana Place Inn
Pinkham Notch, Jackson, New Hampshire
03846

Innkeepers: Betty and Malcolm Jennings
Telephone: 603-383-6822
Rooms: 14, 8 baths to share.
Rates: $14–$26, bed and breakfast.
Facilities: Open all year. Breakfast for house guests. Dinner. Piano Bar. Parking. Swimming. Tennis. Skiing, downhill and cross-country. Fishing.

HOW TO GET THERE:

Take I-93 north to Lincoln turn right on Route 112, Kancamagus Highway to Conway, take Route 16 North past Jackson. The Inn is on the left.

Located at the foot of Mount Washington, surrounded by 600,000 acres of unspoiled National Forest, the Dana Place Inn nestles in a beautiful valley next to the Ellis River. The house was built in the mid-nineteenth century, and surely must have been a stage coach stop. It was a farmhouse, set amid an apple orchard, built by Antwin Dana. Set your own pace amid lawns, gardens, streams, meadows, and woodland trails. Walk through the orchard, past the swimming pool, take the country road past the tennis courts, along a mossy tree-shaded path, through a clearing, and ⬤ there is a crystal clear rock-bound pool in the Ellis River. Peace beyond description.

Skiing is of course, superb here, as well as hiking and mountain climbing for the experienced mountaineer. During school vacations lunch can be had at the Inn, and in all seasons they specialize in picnic lunches. Come home to dinner to wonderful New England food, with more than a sophisticated Continental touch. ⬤ Choose between Iced Gazpacho and Aunt Edna's Crab Bisque. In summer the vegetables come right out of Dana Place's own garden. Betty Jennings' dad has been chef at The New England Inn in Intervale for thirty years so she knows about food and inns.

After a day of skiing the place to unwind is the attractive bar, and enjoy hot buttered rum, hot mulled cider, good cheer and if it is a weekend, the intimate piano music of Mike Jewell.

ℰ: I adore the Patchwork Shop, located right in the Inn, pillows for the Tooth Fairy, precious aprons, just what is needed for a take-home gift.

𝒮: The flower wagon that fills your view from the dining room is charming. Bring your camera.

Whitneys'

Jackson, New Hampshire
03846

Innkeepers: Don Murray, owner, Bob Sullo, Manager
Telephone: 603-383-4291
Rooms: 37, 30 with private baths.
Rates: AP, Deluxe single, $26, per person. Double $24 pp, 3 persons, $23 pp. Standard, Single, $20, Double, $19. Weekly rates on application.
Facilities: Opens early in December, stays open until the snow is gone. Opens latter part of June and stays open until the foliage is gone. Breakfast, Lunch and Dinner served. Bring your own liquor, set-ups provided. TV. Motel rooms accessible for wheelchairs. Swimming in pond. White water canoeing. Skiing. Winter sports.

HOW TO GET THERE:

Take Route 16 north from Conway about 18 miles and turn right. Follow sign to Jackson.

Part of this old Inn was built in the 18th century, and it was enlarged 100 years later, by lifting the original building and erecting a first floor beneath it. It's the truth! Anyway, it has a beautiful location in the White Mountains, with a lovely pond for swimming, and nice grounds for just loafing, and a good restaurant for just eating. In case you want a little more activity, there are weekly cookouts, hikes, a Sunday night buffet, games to play indoors or out. One of the nice things about Whitneys' is the size of its library.

Fishing is close by, so are several places to play golf. Whitneys' really began as a winter place, but summer keeps pushing right in, and they stay open almost all year. A new all weather tennis court adds to the summer fun, and when you have finished a good workout on the court, you can refresh at the lovely new cocktail lounge.

The food is old style Yankee home cooking, with at least two entrees every night. You'll like this homey place. It's a nice place if you have a family, because there are cottages. A real vacation for Mommy, and lots of things for every age youngster to do.

E: I like sports and they have croquet, ping-pong, horse-shoes, badminton and lots more.

S: My favorite fisherman comes all the way from San Francisco to Whitneys' . . . they must be biting here.

> *An unlit hearth in a good tavern is warmer by equators than a blazing fire where there is no love.*

The Arlberg
Laconia-Gilford, New Hampshire
03246

Innkeepers: John and Alyce Rock
Telephone: 603-293-7781
Rooms: 12, 6 with private baths.
Rates: EP, $12 to $20.
Facilities: Breakfast and Dinner served. Dining Room.
Lounge. Ski shop. Heated swimming pool.

HOW TO GET THERE:
The Arlberg Inn is located on Route 11A opposite
the entrance to the Gunstock Ski and Camp Area in
Gilford, 7 miles from downtown Laconia.

If you are longing for a Tyrolean touch to your life, check in at The Arlberg Inn, which is located practically on the Gunstock Ski Area, 20 miles of trails, 5 slopes, 2 double chair lifts, single chair lift, 2 T bars and 2 rope tows with loads of snow. If you need equipment, you can get it at the Ski Shop right in the Inn. Join the group in the Lounge for Apres ski sandwiches and drinks.

The Inn's menu takes you right across the sea to the Austrian Alps with Sauerbraten and Schnitzel a la Holstein. There is also some New England seafood, Stuffed Shrimp, Baked Clams and Oysters. Frogs Legs and Roast Duckling served in an unusual green peppercorn sauce are popular choices.

A summer theatre at Gilford is close by for straw hat entertainment. Lake Winnipesaukee is very close, and you can go antiquing, hiking, wandering, bicycling. Badminton, ping pong, bird and animal watching are offered at the Inn. Or you can just find a shady tree and rest awhile.

E: It may not be Austrian, but I'll choose the famous Grasshopper Pie.

S: Swiss-fried potatoes (Rosti) and Red Cabbage will be my undoing, a very hard choice to make, when the Tenderloin Kabobs and Steak Au Poivre are tempting me too!

> *A glass of good whiskey before an open fire in a good inn is an unspoken toast to life as it should be lived.*

The Inn at Steele Hill
Laconia, New Hampshire
03246

Innkeepers: Jerome and Nancy Walker
Telephone: 603-524-0500
Rooms: 25, all with private bath in main house, additions share.
Rates: MAP Double $20–$30, Single, $25–$38, Dormitory space $15, per person. Various specials. Write for rates.
Facilities: Open all year. Breakfast, Lunch and Dinner served. Bar. TV. Parking. Pond swimming. Own rope tow for skiing. Scenic. Stable.

HOW TO GET THERE:

Take I93 north to Exit 20. Take Route 11 north east to Laconia.

This Inn was built in 1940, as a large country House, on 500 acres of Hill. It has one of the most beautiful locations in the world. The rooms are large, with tile baths, a sprinkler system, big closets, and good lights. There is a wonderful informal feeling, Nancy Walker has a way with people, and also animals. She was mourning the sale of one of her sheep the day we were there. She had promised, so there was no way out. There are cats, and a dog named Lady, horses, and lambs, and even children. One of the great things about this place is the barn, where on those inevitable rainy days, the young can play basketball and other indoor games.

The Inn has its own 9 hole golf course, a lovely pool for swimming, and its own rope tow for skiing. There is a summer theater at Guilford. There is a combo on weekends, so the lounge really swings. For horse people there are horses, and beautiful trails for riding. Also fishing.

The dining room serves good, wholesome American style food, with home baked bread and rolls. Saturday night is Prime Rib Night. A light lunch can be had poolside in summer, and at the recreation area in winter. This is a great place to come with the whole family, but it is also recommended for honeymoons! All right, start a tradition.

&: The view from this Inn is absolutely fantastic!

Our sympathy for the hardships of our forebears should be somewhat mitigated by the fact that they had the best of country inns.

Beal House Inn
Littleton, New Hampshire
03561

Innkeeper: Mrs. Edward Grady
Telephone: 603-444-2661
Rooms: 15, 10 with bath.
Rates: $8 to $10 per person.
Facilities: Open all year. Breakfast *only.* No bar. Set-ups provided. Parking.

HOW TO GET THERE:

Go as far as you can on I91 continue on Route 5 North to Wells River, turn right on Route 302, 26 miles to Littleton. Or from Interstate 93 North, take exit 42. 1 mile north of this exit.

We have made an exception of the Beal House, as it serves only breakfast. The reason is the really superb rooms, all with either canopy or four-poster beds. And most of the antiques in the Inn are for sale, and if that's not enough there's a barn full of more. Mrs. Grady (who used to be Mrs. Beal) has owned and operated this Inn for more than forty years.

Littleton is in the heart of the White Mountains, one of those towns that used to have all kinds of interesting industries, a company that made stereoscopes, another that made foot pedal organs, a silver company, all gone of course.

Mrs. Grady is a real New England lady, she reminds me (Suzy) of my Aunt Margaret, with her white hair and straight back. She runs a tight little ship here, and it is worth an overnight visit when you are in the north country.

Even the riches of Kubla Khan cannot sway the evenhanded hospitality of a proper innkeeper.

Lyme Inn
Lyme, New Hampshire
03768

Innkeepers: Connie and Ray Bergendoff
Telephone: 603-795-2222
Rooms: 15 rooms, 6 baths, 8 with ½ bath.
Rates: Single $11-$17, Double $16-$27.
Facilities: Open all year except last 3 weeks in March, and first 3 weeks in December. Breakfast and Dinner served. Dining room closed on Tuesdays. Bar. Parking. TV. Library. 5 rooms with fireplaces.

HOW TO GET THERE:
Exit 14 from I91, Located on NH 10, on village common.

Everywhere we have been in New England innkeepers have asked us if we know Connie and Ray Bergendoff, who own and run the Lyme Inn. This charming pair from Missouri were bitten by the "inn bug" and looked until they found their dream inn, on the common in Lyme. Connie is an antique dealer, and everything in the Inn is for sale, the antiques, that is. All of the original rooms have been restored very much in keeping with the age of the Inn, built between 1802 and 1809.

The tavern has a great fireplace and on a cold night a cheese fondue is a must. ☞ The fresh spinach-raw mushroom salad is beautiful, and the house salad dressing is, to quote Elizabeth, FAN-tastic! Oysters fried in beer, and Lyme Inn Cheesecake Parfait are two delicious oddities offered. Have you ever heard of putting sauerkraut in Chocolate Cake? Neither had we, but a moister, more delectable devil's food has never come our way.

E: The room that is directly above the Taproom has a chaise lounge and is so pretty and charming. All the rooms are lovely, but this is my favorite.

S: One of our other Innkeepers, Esther Serafini, lived here many years ago when she was a young school teacher. Small world!

The cheers of millions are for politicians, while the quiet appreciation of a well cooked chop is but for a few.

The Edgewood Inn
New London, New Hampshire
03257

Innkeepers: David Seybold and Tom Mills; owner, Murray
    Washburn
Telephone: 603-526-2171
Rooms: 8, 4 with private bath, 4 semi-private.
Rates: $12–$18.
Facilities: Open all year. Lunch, Dinner. Bar. Television.
    Skiing. Paddle Tennis.

HOW TO GET THERE:

From I91 take Exit 8 at Ascutney, Vermont. Follow
signs to Claremont, N.H. Take Route 11 East to Newport, Sunapee, George Mills and New London. There
is bus service via Vermont Transit from Boston.

This is one of our country inns that we recommend for our younger folks. The rooms are small, but ample, and clean. The Inn has a lounge for television and reading.

The tavern, Peter Christian's Tavern, has tables and chairs that are all handmade. ☛ The Tavern itself, walls and beams are from an old barn in Vermont. Hand-hewn! The Tavern serves only beer and wine. The menu has cheeses, interesting sandwiches, soups, salad and desserts, not really a full dinner, just enough. ☛They grow their own vegetables at the Inn.

An added plus is the sometimes appearance of Garry Robinson, a classical guitar player, and so good.

E: I like the stew, served in a mug.

S: The Artisan's Workshop is right there.

Start my day with a real New England breakfast and I can lick the world.

H ide-Away Lodge
New London, New Hampshire
03257

Innkeepers: Lilli and Wolf Heinberg
Telephone: 603-526-4861
Rooms: 8 with bath.
Rates: $17 double; $48 double MAP; $24 single MAP.
Weekly rates MAP $300 double; $150 single.
Facilities: Open mid-May to mid-October. Fishing and
Swimming on Lake Sunapee, a short walk away.
Golf on 3 courses, excellent Tennis nearby. Summer
theatre.

HOW TO GET THERE:
Fly to Lebanon, New Hampshire and be picked up
and delivered to the Inn. Or by car, 90 miles from
Boston, 240 from NYC. Follow Main Street past Colby-
Sawyer College to blinker light at north end of town.
Go straight ahead and follow the signs about 2 miles
from town.

There has to be an exception to every rule and Hide-Away Lodge is ours. Only open five months we feel, does not qualify an inn for our book . . . until now. We know you will agree with us. There was no way we could not include Hide-Away Lodge.

When we drove in to this lovely old house and met the host, Wolf Heinberg, who has a most engaging smile, we knew we had found something special. We already had heard about the food served here and after talking with Wolf we were sure all we had heard was true. Thankfully we were able to stay, the last room in the Inn.

Dinner hour arrived and we went down to the cocktail lounge, The Pipedreaming Pub. We placed a cocktail order, drooled over the menu, and ordered dinner and the wine list. Wolf suggested that maybe a look in the wine cellar would help us decide. We followed him into a huge temperature controlled wine cellar. Fantastic, every wall covered with wine; in the center of the room, a huge table with silver candelabras and a beautiful wine book. We chose one after much looking. Wolf is a very proud man and he should be.

We finished our cocktail and were called to dinner. I had cold spinach soup and Suzy had Paté, both superb. The salad was perfect . . . spinach again for me and mushrooms for Suzy. We could go on and on, everything we ate was so good, everything about the Inn so exceptional. All the people who help run it, and of course, hats off to Lilli and Wolf Heinberg. As if this were not enough, there are bits of poetry all over the Inn written by Wolf. You must come and try it. But call ahead, reservations are a must.

E: I wanted to stay in the wine cellar.

S: I just wanted to stay.

New London Inn
New London, New Hampshire
03257

Innkeepers: Lois and Frank B. Conklin
Telephone: 603-526-2791
Rooms: 25, all with baths.
Rates: $16–$25, tax included.
Facilities: Open all year. Breakfast, Lunch and Dinner. Main
Dining Room, Coffee Shop, Cocktail Lounge. TV.
Parking. Skiing. Two public beaches nearby. (Break-
fast only meal served Christmas Day.)

HOW TO GET THERE:

Take Exit 8 at Ascutney, Vermont on I91, follow signs
to Claremont, N.H. Take Route 11 east to Newport,
Sunapee, Georges Mills and New London. There is
bus service via Vermont Transit from Boston to New
London, and from White River Junction, Vermont, to
New London.

This inn, which has been serving the traveler since 1792, is blooming anew under the direction of the Conklins, who bought it in 1967. Frank was at Deerfield Academy for years, so things antique are nothing new to him.

New London is the home of Colby Sawyer College. There is always a lot going on at the college. Also, the New London Barn Players is the oldest summer theater in New Hampshire.

This is a family operated Inn. The number one cook, Sue Hoyt, is good, and has a well-trained staff. The lady who meets you at the desk also doubles as dining room hostess. You'll feel at home in no time.

The rooms are nice, large, comfortable, most of them with cross ventilation, and louvered doors. The dining room has recently been done over, and there is a nice little coffee shop if you are in a hurry. But why anyone should have to hurry in this most relaxed part of the world we really don't know.

There has never been a better day than this, for I have had a good night's rest.

The Scottish Lion
North Conway, New Hampshire
03860

Innkeepers: Jack and Judy Hurley
Telephone: 603-356-2482
Rooms: 8, 4 with private bath, others share.
Rates: $10.00 per person for bed and breakfast.
Facilities: Open all year. Breakfast for house guests. Lunch
in summer. Dinner. Bar. Parking. Scottish Gift Shop.
Red Lion Art Gallery.

HOW TO GET THERE:
Take Route 16 from Conway, then Route 302 to North
Conway.

This delightful bit of Scotland is run by a charming young pair, Jack and Judy Hurley. Parts of the house were built in 1780, and as in all old inns, there is still building going on, a lovely deck for summer luncheons has just been finished. The Black Watch Pub has some fantastic Scottish military paintings, large sweeping battle scenes. There are three dining rooms, but the St. Andrews room will appeal to all golfers. The waitresses are clad in kilts, and charming lassies they are.

There is so much to do in the Washington Valley, the gateway to the White Mountains; sports, entertainment, shopping and dining. North Conway is a lovely little town. There is a beautiful gift shop right in the Inn, with imported woolens, crystal, jewelry, and food (shortbread for one).

In the far corner of the Inn's field, is a new art gallery. Designed with intentions of being the "best commerical gallery north of Boston," the gallery is built in the shape of an octagonal star in order to give maximum display of paintings and sculpture.

Bed and breakfast is offered, in the Scottish manner, a really hearty, full breakfast, other meals are extra. Drinks and dinner by one of the old fireplaces is a joy, and if you are lucky you may glimpse the small daughter of the house on her way to bed.

E: When you come down the road and see the magnificent flag streaming out in the wind you just can't go on by. Stop for a drink if you can't stay the night, you'll love it.

S: Call for reservations. This place is small, and you don't want to miss it.

Wells Wood
Plainfield, New Hampshire
03781

Innkeepers: Mr. and Mrs. J. Thomas Wells
Telephone: 603-675-5360
Rooms: 4, 2 with private bath, 2 that share.
Rates: $21.50–$48.50 with continental breakfast.
Facilities: Closed on Monday. Breakfast for house guests
only. Dinner. Bar. Television.

HOW TO GET THERE:

Exit from I91 at Ascutney, north to Route 5. Turn
right at the light in Windsor, over covered bridge, north
on 12A to Wells Wood. The sign is on the left. Or Exit
20 from I89, south on 12A 8½ miles. Sign on right.

What a magical place is Wells Wood. Mr. and Mrs. Wells have taken Maxfield Parrish's home and studio, and his machine shop, and turned them into a fairy tale retreat overlooking a magnificent valley. The trees are old and gnarled, there are beautiful shallow pools, settings that once served as backgrounds for Parrish's fanciful paintings. Mr. Wells is an interior designer, and the master suite shows his distinctive touch. The massive candelabra on the bar, and the sconces behind it, are European pieces brought back by the Wellses from their annual trips to the Continent. There is a charming antique shop in what once was the machine shop.

Meals in the splendid dining hall are as lush as the surroundings. Mrs. Wells, an opera singer, is also a star in the kitchen, desserts being her special forte. Chocolate Mousse Cake, English Trifle, great huge sundaes, or Café Ambassador, a lyric of hot coffee, a scoop of ice cream, topped with whipped cream flavored with Napoleon Brandy are but a few ways to end a meal.

The fireplaces and inglenooks glow with the warmth of open fires when the winds sweep down the Connecticut River Valley. There are 20 good ski slopes just minutes away, and much to amuse a guest, whatever the season. Fifty wooded acres surround this lovely Inn, beckoning you for a walk.

The small son of the house is named Jason, and there is a very large friendly dog. Be sure to make reservations because you wouldn't want to miss this charmer.

E: The large copper curiosity in the bar began life as a towel warmer in a barber shop. This place is filled with things, strange and marvelous to see.

S: The steps that lead up to nowhere beside the library fireplace, the view from the windows in the great hall, the mysterious aura that pervades the Inn, all fascinate me.

The Homestead
Sugar Hill, New Hampshire
03585

Innkeepers: Esther Serafini, Barbara Serafini Hayward
Telephone: 603-823-5564 or 9577
Rooms: 10 rooms in main house, each with running water, sharing 4 baths, 7 rooms with private baths in house across the street.
Rates: MAP, $16–$22 per person.
Facilities: Open every day from Memorial Day till after Thanksgiving. Breakfast and Dinner served. No bar.

HOW TO GET THERE:

Take Exit 38 from I93, to Route 117. The Homestead is about 3 miles up the hill on Route 117. Or coming from the west turn east on Route 117 from Route 302.

If you want to hear tales of Old New Hampshire, and stay in a country inn that was built in 1802, and is owned by a direct descendant of the first settler, go up Sugar Hill to The Homestead. Don't be fooled by the name Serafini, Esther Tefft Serafini met him when she was teaching school and he was at Univ. of N.H. Her family has been running the Inn since they took their first "summer boarders" in 1881. Esther made her first "tip" when she was 10, wanting to be like the big girls, she was allowed to pass the relish tray.

The antiques in the Inn are fabulous. You can sleep in the four poster bed used by Moses Aldrich himself, it came up on the first ox cart from Richmond, N.H., with his wife Sarah riding on top of the load. Some of the recipes used for the Inn's wonderful food are more than 150 years old.

Esther Serafini believes in breakfasts, and she serves something in the fall she calls a "Harvest Breakfast," you could scythe a whole field on half of what she serves. Her Thanksgiving Dinners are famous from here to California, one family flew in for the holiday weekend from there, felt it was a bargain, even with the plane fare.

Esther does about half the cooking. The other half is done by a lady who came for the weekend 32 years ago and is still there. Something called "Best Ever Pie" is a favorite on the menu, and Esther had just finished putting up 60 quarts of rhubarb the last time we were there. There is usually only one entree, except on Fridays, when there is meat or fish. But always *six* desserts, homemade ice cream, homemade rolls, and other old-fashioned temptations.

Don't put off your trip to Sugar Hill, this is a country inn creeper's country inn.

&: Esther's book, Tales and Tours and Taste Treats of the White Mountains and Sugar Hill, gives tours, history and recipes.

S: If I am missing, look for me at The Homestead.

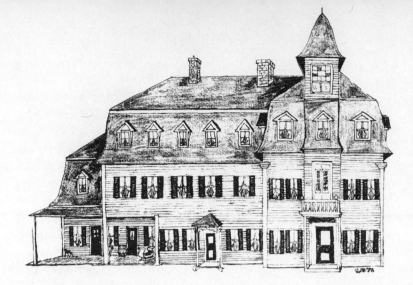

Tamworth Inn
Tamworth, New Hampshire
03886

Innkeepers: The McCarthy Family
Telephone: 603-323-7721
Rooms: 21 rooms; 10 with private bath, others share.
Rates: EP: Single $5 to $10, Double $12 to $21. AP rates
  on request.
Facilities: Open all year. Breakfast, Lunch and Dinner in
  summer and fall. Breakfast and Dinner in winter and
  spring. Snack Bar. Cocktail Lounge. Swimming pool.
  Trout stream. Gift shop. Summer theatre across the
  street. Tennis, golf and horseback riding close by for
  summer, skiing and snowshoeing in winter.

HOW TO GET THERE:
From Route 93, take Route 104, to Route 25, to Route
113. Or if approaching from Route 95, take Route 16
to 25 to 113.

If trout fishing is your sport, you will find a ☞ beautiful stream at the bottom of the Tamworth Inn's garden. The Inn building itself, is very old, middle-aged, and young, having been added to, restored and remodeled. The McCarthy Family has been in residence here since 1973, three generations of them, all working to make the Inn warm and welcoming. Grandmother Rudder does the cooking, an uncle tends bar. Fresh parsley and herbs are grown by Grandfather, and the faraway grandmother in Pennsylvania sends handmade articles to sell in the quaint gift shop. The young sons of the Innkeepers have not minded being transplanted from Pennsylvania, there are so many activities for youngsters here. No time to be bored, hiking trails, bicycling, fishing, riding and tennis are close at hand. In winter there is skiing, cross country and downhill, skating and snowshoeing. ☞ Walk across the street to the summer theater.

Tamworth is one of the picture book villages of New England. The clock in the church tower still chimes the hour, and though you are away from the mainstream of traffic, you are minutes away from the many attractions nature offers here near Lake Winnepesaukee. Prices are moderate at this dear old Inn, so come often and stay long.

℘: Winston Tibbs, a really distinguished Persian cat is one of the owners of this caravanserai. If you scratch his tummy he will roll over and purr.

The Playhouse Inn
Whitefield, New Hampshire
03598

Innkeepers: Lucienne and Noel Lacan
Telephone: 603-837-2527
Rooms: 12, 8 with private bath, others share.
Rates: MAP: Single, $20-$28 Double, $18-$22 per person. EP, $10-$24.
Facilities: Open 7 days July and August, with Breakfast, Lunch, and Dinner. Closed Monday during spring and fall, Dinner only. Swimming Pool, Beer Garden, Cocktail Lounge with Cabaret Show during July & August, as well as Summer Stock Theatre. Golf and Tennis 5 minutes away.

HOW TO GET THERE:

Take Interstate 93, then US Route 3 into Whitefield.

198

With the Weathervane Theater just across the lawn, Lucienne and Noel Lacan have taken the playhouse theme for their delightful country inn. Noel is the chef, and the menu from the Prelude through the Curtain Calls proves it, in every scene and every act.

The new swimming pool, with its view of the mountains, is lovely. Whitefield is full of great big summer hotels, famous the world over, but closed down tight in winter. The Playhouse Inn is open all year, so come snow or sunshine, you will find a welcome there. There are six fireplaces in this comfortable old house.

From the Backstage Bar, to the Limelighter Restaurant, the theatrical touch is there, but with a really solid Gallic base.

E: The menu is great! "Snails en surprise" have a new approach, and to finish off with Flaming *Spanish* coffee is indeed a switch.

S: There are those who hate vegetables, and then there's me. Endives Meuniere, Braised Heart of Celery, Lima Bean Bretonne, Mushrooms Sauteed Provencale... who needs meat?

> *Were it not for a night's rest in a country inn tomorrow would be but another day.*

The Windrifter Inn
Wolfeboro, New Hampshire
03894

Innkeeper: Steve Ross
Telephone: 603-569-4800
Rooms: 13 rooms in inn, all but 3 with private bath.
Rates: $20.50 to $22.50, plus motel units which accommodate
a family of 4.
Facilities: Lunch and Dinner served. TV. Parking. Bar.
Supper club. Swimming pool. Golf course adjacent.

HOW TO GET THERE:
Wolfeboro is located at the eastern end of Lake Winnipesaukee, on Route 28.

The old house that is The Windrifter Inn was built in 1775, was owned in the nineteenth century by the patent medicine queen Lydia Pinkham, and first became an inn in 1904.

This is a good country Inn for families, there's so much to do, so close at hand. Wolfeboro is right in the center of New Hampshire, and a free boat launch at Wolfeboro gives access to Lake Winnipesaukee's 72 square miles. Swim in the lovely pool, spend the day on the adjacent golf course, ski in winter, go ice fishing or skating.

The old barn has been turned into the largest nightclub in the area, with music every night and "big name entertainers" on weekends. If you are looking for some sophisticated night life, you might find it here.

The menu is varied enough to please the fussiest eater, lobster four different ways, steak, prime ribs, and kidney lamb chops, double thick. There's a nice bay window in the dining room, so tuck yourself away and settle down to a night of comfort at The Windrifter Inn.

When life dwindles thin and you wonder if the sun will rise on another day, seek perhaps an unfamiliar but rejuvenating bed in a nearby country inn.

The Bethel Inn
Bethel, Maine
04217

Innkeeper: Owner, Barry Harris; Manager, Ernie Tremblay Jr.

Telephone: 207-824-2175

Rooms: 65, all with private bath.

Rates: In season, EP, $22-$58; off season MAP $22 double, $31 single.

Facilities: Open almost all year. Closed November 1-20, and April 15-May 15. Breakfast. Lunch. Dinner. Bar. Parking. Golf. Tennis, Swimming. Cross-country Skiing at door. ✈ Helicopter Pad. Elevator.

HOW TO GET THERE:

Bethel is located at the intersection of U.S. Route 2 and Maine Routes 5, 26 and 35. From the south take Exit 11 off the Maine Turnpike at Gray and follow Route 26 to Bethel. The Inn is located on the Village Green.

Rejoice! The Bethel Inn has been restored to its former glory. Mowed and manicured, polished and perfect, the Inn is truly the gem of New England inns. Set on the green in the quaint village of Bethel, the Inn supplies every creature comfort known to man. Vacation four seasons of the year, take it blissfully easy, or join in the fun and games. You really don't need a car, ➤ you can walk everywhere in the town, shop in the dear little shops, and though you feel you are at the end of the world, the Inn has twenty-four hour telephone service to keep you in touch.

Many of the guests have been coming here for years and years, as an overnight stop on the way north, or for the month or season. The Bethel Inn is the sort of place we can't do without, and why should we, with Barry Harris in control? Lovely rooms, good food, convivial companionship in the attractive bar, keep us coming back.

E: Happiness is finding an owner like ➤ Barry Harris who does everything right, even flying.

S: Long a favorite vacation spot of my parents this dear old Inn still has everything anyone could want for a real Down East vacation.

> *Having had an excellent meal and a lovely evening, I tucked myself in bed knowing I had sinned but it did not seem to matter.*

The Sudbury Inn
Bethel, Maine
04217

Innkeepers: The Gasser Family
Telephone: 207-824-2174
Rooms: 17, 5 baths.
Rates: $18–$22, bed and breakfast.
Facilities: Closed Monday. Closed 3 weeks in April, 3 weeks in November. Lunch served from Memorial Day to October 31. Dinner all year. Bar. Television. Parking. Live entertainment weekends. Skiing. Swimming in the Sunday River. Canoeing.

HOW TO GET THERE:
Leave I-95 at Exit 11 (Gray) and take Maine Route 26 north to Bethel.

This relaxing, family run village Inn is the ideal place for the family vacation. Children are welcome here, the Gassers have several little ones of their own. Bethel, located in the quiet western mountains of Maine where the White Mountains begin, is a delightful town. This one hundred year old Inn welcomes you with open arms.

A bright fire when the weather crisps up cheers the traveller. Wander on into the Ploughman's Rest Lounge and have a sip from the cup that never fails to please. This is a lively weekend spot. Friday nights in summer, Saturday night in winter, a variety of live entertainment is offered.

The nearby Sunday River is great for canoeing or swimming. The countryside is lush in late spring, fishermen, hikers, picnickers, and nature lovers find everything they want not too far away. The skies seem clearer up here away from pollution, bluer during the day, more star spangled by night. Autumn paints a wild picture of the woods. Be sure to reserve a room ahead of time, this is the busiest season of them all.

𝓔: Put another nickel in, in the Nickelodeon, and give me music, music, music!

𝓢: The dining room, with its warm red ceiling and the quaint wallpaper has been the scene of some memorable meals.

You cannot hide a good country inn.

The Thistle Inn
Boothbay Harbor, Maine
04538

Innkeeper: Leonie Greenwood-Adams
Telephone: 207-633-3541
Rooms: 10 rooms, 1 with private bath, others share.
Rates: Single from $8 to $12, double from $12 to $18.
Facilities: Open all year. Lunch and Dinner served. Bar. TV. Downtown location.

HOW TO GET THERE:

Take Route 95 to Route 1. Continue on Route 1 to Route 27 which will take you into Boothbay Harbor.

Thistle Inn is an old sea captain's house, that has been turned into a great, raggle-taggle country inn, whose owner Leonie Greenwood-Adams has to be one of the all time fantastic characters on the Maine coast. In winter, the lobstermen come in and yarn away the time, ➤ leaning on the dory that serves as a bar. The player piano nearby is totally covered with liquor labels, and the top is crowded with music rolls. Mrs. Greenwood-Adams welcomes children and pets, if both are well behaved. No breakfast is served because no one in their right mind gets up for breakfast.

The Mary Queen of Scots Room is for candle-lit dining, the pewter candlesticks are worth the trip up to the Harbor. Informal dining in the horse stalls, and Harness rooms, and drinking in the Old Dory Pub are a year round affair. Traveler, Wayfarer and Refined Persons are welcome at this inn! The Thistle Inn is inclined to be a bit boisterous and overcrowded any Saturday night in mid-summer. Often the noise level gets high, and if you are looking for a quiet place to sleep, this isn't it.

There is a very Scots flavor to the Inn. Mrs. Greenwood-Adams' former husband, the late Donald Morren, was a Scotsman, and they created the Inn and the highland atmosphere together.

Mrs. Greenwood-Adams' father came from Australia, and is commemorated by a drink called the Boomerang. Things on the menu have fascinating names, T'Donald's Scottish Lobster Pie, Edinburgh Style Potato Salad, Kingdom of Fife Pie, Robbie Burns Steak, and Scottish Sherry Trifle, cheek by jowl with the Indian Pudding.

E: The Dory Bar is really unique, with a list of drinks that makes me want to stay and sample a few, The Boomerang, which is milk, Scotch and Creme de Cacao, Shandy Gaff, Pims #1 Cup, Thistle Rob Roy, and a Scottish Mule.

S: A little bit of Britain, pub-style, or country inn, transplanted to the coast of Maine. The Thistle Inn must be seen to be believed.

Winter's Inn
Kingfield, Maine
04947

Innkeeper: Michael Thom
Telephone: 207-265-5421
Rooms: 16, 7 with private bath, others share.
Rates: Summer EP $8–$14 per person. Winter EP $10–$20 per person. Rates include Continental Breakfast and are based on double occupancy. MAP and special group rates on request.
Facilities: Open almost all year. Closed from end of ski season, generally late April, through May and June, and from October 21 to early December. Breakfast, Lunch and Dinner served daily. Dining room, outside terrace dining, fireside cocktail lounges, intimate bar, live classical music weekends. Tennis. Swimming pool. Skiing. Bus service to mountain and from nearby airports upon request.

HOW TO GET THERE:

Take Maine Turnpike to Exit 12, continue on Route 4 to Farmington, then Route 27 to Kingfield. Midway between Montreal or Quebec City on the way to the Maine coast.

Located in the heart of the western Maine mountains, including Bigelow, Sugarloaf, and Saddleback, Winter's Inn is a restored Neo-Georgian manor house sitting on top of a ten acre hill on the edge of town. Built at the turn of the century for Amos Greene Winter, the house had fallen into sad disrepair, until it was rescued in 1972 by Michael Thom, a young architect from Cambridge, Massachusetts, and Toronto, Canada. ➤ Much to his pride, the house has now been listed on the National Register of Historic Places.

Elegant, without being stiff or pretentious, the Inn has been decorated with ➤ handsome wallpapers. The walls are hung with a fine collection of oil paintings, and gold framed mirrors. The view from the dining room windows of the western mountains is breathtaking. The view is the same from the swimming pool.

➤ The food served in Le Papillon is delightful, a continuing surprise in this far away Inn at the back of beyond. Recent guests spent their days climbing mountains, came home to the Inn for a swim and a drink, dressed for dinner and dined elegantly, the best of both worlds.

Hunting, fishing, hiking (the Appalachian Trail comes up this way) and canoeing welcome the outdoor types. The downhill skier is especially happy here, but so is the lady guest ensconced by the pool with her needlepoint or a book.

E: There lives here an Inn cat, Balthazar. He is orange and white and as regal as his name. Once I had a look-a-like cat, Alleycat, just as majestic.

S: Do you know another inn where guests are welcomed by the gentle music of the harpsichord (often live, by the chef)? Pause awhile and listen to the past.

The Old Village Inn
Ogunquit, Maine
03907

Innkeepers: Frederic L. Thomas and Alf B. Kristiansen
Telephone: 207-646-7088
Rooms: 12, 4 with private bath.
Rates: $18 double with private bath, $14 without. $2 less in winter.
Facilities: Breakfast and Dinner. Bar never closes. In winter no meals on Monday and Tuesday. TV in parlor.

HOW TO GET THERE:
Near the center of the Village at 30 Main Street.

In the last five years Fred Thomas and Alf Kristiansen have resurrected a typical in-village inn that has a history going back to 1833. Interestingly part of its history was that on the August 2, 1942 issue of the *Saturday Evening Post*, the Inn was the subject of a John Falter cover.

Hard on the rockbound coast of Maine, Ogunquit has interests for all: the famous Ogunquit Playhouse, the newer off-Broadway repertory theatre, swimming, fishing, and of great interest, two unusual walking trails. The Marginal Way winds you along the spectacular bay and sea, and the Trolley Trail follows an abandoned line through the woods.

The rooms are plain but comfortable, and one has a headboard made from four ladderback chairs. According to Fred, its the only one of its kind, and he should know, because he invented it.

The bar will whisk you right into the best of English country pubs complete to the stemmed hanging glasses, and the cooking unit behind the bar. The dining rooms spill out onto the porches in clement weather for a restful informality.

£: The bar makes me want to sip all day, and by the way, the coffee table in front of the fireplace has a most unusual collection of glass paperweights.

S: When an innkeeper takes the time and effort to personally make shades and valances to match the wallpaper in the Bird and Bottle Room, he has my heart.

Insomnia is almost a blessing if you are in an inn within easy earshot of a country church bell.

The East Wind Inn
Tenants Harbor, Maine
04860

Innkeepers: Tim Watts and Ginny Wheeler
Telephone: 207-372-8800
Rooms: 16, 6 baths, 1 suite with private bath.
Rates: $18 single, $24 double.
Facilities: Open 7 days a week, all year. Breakfast, Lunch and Dinner. Service Bar. Telephones in rooms. Deep water anchorage for boats.

HOW TO GET THERE:
From U.S. Route 1, just east of Thomaston, take State Route 131 south 9.5 miles to Tenants Harbor. Turn left at the Post Office and continue straight to the Inn.

Have you dreamed of a place that hasn't changed in 85 years, where you can let the children roam around town, fish off the wharf, watch the fishermen unload their gear? Load up the bicycles and head for Tenants Harbor. Tim Watts, the Innkeeper who restored this gem, has lived nearby most of his young life, watched the old white frame house deteriorate, and dreamed of restoring it so others could share the charm of "The Country of the Pointed Firs."

This Inn, open every day all year, is one of the few where you can arrive by boat, find showers available, a laundry room and a 🐟 beauty parlor to repair the ravages of wind and sea.

The Inn is within walking distance of the village where you will find a library, shops, post office and sometimes church suppers on the weekend. Bicycle around the St. George peninsula, find beaches, rock cliffs, tidal pools, old cemeteries, go down to Port Clyde, a fishing village, take the ferry to Monhegan Island. Ski in winter at the Camden Snow Bowl, far from the crowded slopes.

The Inn itself, built in 1890, had stood vacant for more than 20 years. Tim found the owner and persuaded her to sell it to him, and he has fully and lovingly restored it. Hearty, home-cooked New England vittles are served three times a day in the spick-and-span dining room with a glorious harbor view. The Swiss Chocolate Pie is sinfully good.

E: The freshest seafood is always available at the Inn, and if you want some packed in ice to carry home with you, step next door to the Cod.

S: The wide verandas that cover three sides of the Inn tempt me to spend a long lazy afternoon just rocking gently, doing absolutely *nothing*.

New Meadows Inn
West Bath, Maine
04530

Innkeeper: Richard J. Armstrong
Telephone: 207-443-3921
Rooms: 10, all with bath. Cottage units also available.
Rates: Single, $9.75, Double, $14.50-$28.50.
Facilities: Closed Christmas Day. Breakfast, Lunch and Dinner served. TV in each room. Bar. Parking. Fireplace in lower dining room.

HOW TO GET THERE:
Take New Meadows Road Exit off Route 1. Follow signs to Inn on New Meadows Road.

Richard Armstrong has been at the helm here at New Meadows Inn for the last 18 years, and the Inn has been here for lots longer than that. Bath, Maine, is world renowned for her Bath Built Ships, The Bath Iron works, from Pearl Harbor to the end of World War II delivered 82 destroyers. The entire Japanese nation during this same period built 63 destroyers! Beginning in 1607, and continuing up to the present, Bath men have been turning out ships that go down to the seas, J. P. Morgan's *Corsair*, a four master called *Shenandoah*, built in 1890, we could go on and on. Come to Bath and see the Bath Marine Museum. The museum has loaned a few of their treasures to Mr. Armstrong to display in his establishment.

The dining rooms here are noted for the "Shore Dinners" served. Mr. Armstrong is particularly happy with the success of his new ➤salad bar, he says that the whole atmosphere of the restaurant has changed. People are happier, more relaxed. His immaculate tiled kitchen turns out some excellent food.

The River Room looks out on one of the clean rivers of our not very clean world. This is a real country inn, a stopping place by the side of the road for the traveller. If you are interested in ships, out shopping for a yacht or a dinghy, why don't you try Bath?

"Age appears to be best in four things, old wood best to burn, old wine to drink, old friends to trust, and old inns to enjoy."

Anonymous. Found on a wine list at the John Hancock Inn, Hancock, New Hampshire.

Stage Neck Inn
York Harbor, Maine
03911

Innkeepers: Frances and Alexander (Pud) Warrick
Telephone: 207-363-3850
Rooms: 56, all with bath, private porch, color TV, telephone.
Rates: In season, MAP single $50 to $60; Double $74 to $84.
Off season, EP Single $30 to $40; Double $38 to $48.
Other meal plans, package plans and residential plans
available on request.
Facilities: Closed from early November to late April. Open
the rest of the year. Restaurant. Tap Room. Break-
fast, Lunch and Dinner. Elevator. Wheelchair ac-
cessibility to whole Inn. Swimming. Sailing. Fishing.
Golf. Tennis. Parking. Marina.

HOW TO GET THERE:
2½ miles via Route 1A from Exit 1 on the Maine Turnpike. Take I-95 north from Boston. It is less than 2 hours
from Worcester via 495.

Come to where the river meets the sea, the view from this Inn on the rocky coast of Maine is breathtakingly beautiful. Most of the rooms have a ⬛ water view, ocean, river or harbor, each has its own porch. Stage Neck has much to offer. The swimming pool is filled with warm salt water, for the less hardy types; the Maine ocean water is still as cold as it ever was. If you should come cruising along the coast in your boat, or even one that belongs to someone else, you will find a welcome here. You can dine in the Tap Room if you are informally clad, on the same delicious victuals that are served in the main dining room.

The walk along the cliffs is as scenic as only Maine can be. In the fall the foliage is spectacular, and in this part of Maine there are lots of country fairs.

The Inn offers European and American delicacies. The ⬛ staff is well trained. The grog department will make whatever you desire to drink. There is weekend dancing. Put it all together with the incomparable coast of Maine and you have a perfect Inn.

Would you believe a shop called Tatterdemalion? It is right in the Inn. There is needlepoint with a rainbow of wools, stuffed animals and unusual shell-studded hurricane lamps. Come and see.

E: The rooms are beautifully appointed. You hate to leave.

S: Lunch at poolside is my idea of summer delight. When the pool is warm then I am truly in heaven.

Spring flowers adding the final brush strokes at the edges of the granite, walk to the inn's front stoop.

And a Special Exception For Maine....

While throughout the "Guide" we have hewn strictly to the line and listed only inns that are open all year (or most of the year), Maine, with what could euphemistically be called its unique winter climate, presented a problem. There are some charming inns ... true inns ... that just cannot stay open all year.

As an example we ran across one lady who was still smiling bravely out on one of those fingers that stick into the sea, who had opened her inn the first of May and saw her first guest on the first of July.

SO ... here are some briefer descriptions of inns we like that are certainly worth visiting when they are open.

AND ... if we have missed a Maine inn that does stay open all year, as well we might have, we will rectify it in our next edition.

Spruce Point Inn, Boothbay Harbor, Maine, 04538. Innkeepers: John and Charlotte Druce. Telephone: 207-633-4152. 55 rooms, 55 baths, 12 fireplaces. Open June 15 to September 15. MAP, single $38-$48, double $68-$78, suites, $74-$84. Cottages. Write for rates. TV. 2 pools, 3 tennis courts, Boating, Moorings. You might call this a summer resort, but the country inn feel is really here. Once you drive through the gates onto the peninsula that *is* Spruce Point, you are away from the workaday world. The Druces have been running things here for 17 years, and they know what they're up to. Sunday night there is a cruise around the Harbor with pastries and coffee. Monday morning a cookout breakfast, places for viewing the sunset or the moonrise. E. says you must see the bar, most unique idea for a boater's heaven that's ever crossed her bows.

Whitehall Inn, Camden, Maine 04843. Innkeepers: Ed and Jean Dewing and family. Telephone: 207-236-3391. 38 rooms, 34 baths. Open June 1 through October. Breakfast, and Dinner served. Lunch to house guests. Bar. Parking. For 70 summers there have been guests at Whitehall Inn. The Dewings are new at innkeeping, but believe in all the old traditions, from fingerbowls to the beds turned down at night. Camden is a beautiful, interesting town. Poetess Edna

St. Vincent Millay stood up in the parlor in this house and recited her long poem "Renascence" to the guests. Her high school diploma is framed on the wall, here is where she began. There is a telescope for watching boats in the bay, and comfort unknown on the busy highways.

Newagen Inn, Newagen, Maine, 04552. Innkeeper: Joseph Flood. Telephone: 207-633-5242. 70 rooms, 70 baths, telephones. Bar, TV, Parking, Fireplace. Open mid-June to mid-September, Orchestra Saturday nights. This lovely world away in time was founded in 1923 by Joshua Brooks, and his spirit still lingers. There is a sun-tempered salt water pool, and beautiful, lovely silence. 400 acres of spruces, wooded trails and rocky cove-studded shore surround the Inn. The Inn operates under the European Plan, $25 to $45 a room, and the Modified American Plan, $24 to $35 per person. There is a sweet lady who is described as an unobtrusive director of activities, we think this means she will help you find a fourth at bridge.

Two Village Square, Ogunquit, Maine, 03907. Innkeepers: Richard Bair and Ken Kendrick. Telephone: 207-646-2776. 9 rooms, 2 baths. Open mid-May to mid-November. Cocktail Lounge, Bar and dancing. Summer rates, single $16; double $24–$28. Spring and fall rates, single $13; double $17–$21. Near Ogunquit Playhouse. Located in the center of the village, the Inn sits high on a hill overlooking the ocean. It is an old sea captain's house and is furnished with antiques and European objects of art. The dining rooms are furnished in the same way, with sterling silver, antique Limoges china, Rose Medallion, Steuben and Baccarat crystal. You will find the bar and cocktail lounge very cozy with fireplace and piano. Try to get a room on the third floor, because then you can see the greatest bathroom we have ever seen. Go to Two Village Square in Ogunquit.

Black Point Inn, Prout's Neck Maine, 04070. Innkeeper: Henry C. Petteys. Telephone: 207-883-4311. 75 rooms, 71 with private bath. Open from end of June until after Labor Day. Breakfast, Lunch and Dinner served. Bar. TV. Elevator. Parking. AP, single $46 to $50; double, $78–$98. Leave Maine Turnpike at Exit 7. Go east to Route 1. Turn right on Route 1, go south 2 and 7/10 miles to Route 207.

Turn left on Route 207 and go 5 miles to the Inn. Fly Northeast Airlines to Portland, 11 miles from the Inn. Inn car will meet guests upon advance notice for a nominal charge. One of the most delightful, best managed, beautiful places, and open such a short season. Go. 🐟 The poolside luncheon, with pleasant *live* music is one of the most imaginative, delicious buffets we have encountered anywhere in our travels. The serene, spacious dining room, the welcoming living room, the lovely rooms are just the bare bones of this garden spot.

Rock Gardens Inn, Sebasco, Maine, 04565. Innkeepers: Dot and Gene Winslow. Telephone: 207-389-1339. 4 rooms in main Inn, 9 cottages, all with bath. Fireplaces in cottages. Breakfast, Lunch and Dinner served. No bar. Bring your own. Open mid-June to late September. Rates: $23 to $34 per person. Keep on going beyond the Sebasco Lodge, and you will come to Rock Gardens Inn, on a rocky point sticking out into the Atlantic. Life is informal here, but if you like a lovely garden come and stay awhile. The Winslows have been running the place for 33 years. There's one entree at night, but if you *can't* have lobster, there will be something else. It was Pot Roast the night we were there, for the nonlobster eaters. It smelled delicious.

Migis Lodge, South Casco, on Sebago Lake, Maine, 04077. Innkeepers: Gene and Grace Porta. Telephone: 207-655-4524. 6 rooms in main Inn, 25 cottages, all with private baths. Fireplaces all over. Open late May, close mid-October. $22 to $34 per person, American Plan. 90 acres with trails through the woods, on a sparkling lake. The names of the cottages give you a clue, Moonrise, Spruce, Driftwood and Skylark, are only a few. They are charming, with the gay patchwork quilts used as spreads, 🐟 fresh fruit in each room, and two great people getting and keeping this all together, Gene and Grace Porta. 🐟 All boating (except motor) is free for guests, there is marvelous fishing, Water skiing is scheduled daily, and there are just loads of wonderful, relaxing things to do. Wednesday afternoon there is a cookout on an island.

The Squire Tarbox House, RD2, Westport Island, Wiscasset, Maine, 04578. Innkeeper: Eleanor Harriman Smith. Telephone: 207-882-7693. 7 rooms, 5 baths. Fireplaces in every room. Open May 1, close October 15. Breakfast, Lunch and Dinner. No bar, bring your own. TV. Parking. $25 for double room with continental breakfast. Here is a local lady, born right on the island, who restored this 1763 house in 1955. The wainscoting in one of the downstairs bedrooms is *one* piece of wood. If you come in June there are banks of lupin to regard while terrace-sitting. Wiscasset, known as the prettiest village in Maine, is the nearest town. Mrs. Smith and her sister, Mrs. Wright, once had a well-known restaurant called The Summer Kitchen, now their cooking is confined to the needs of house guests, and outsiders by reservations. This is country living at its best.

Homewood Inn, Yarmouth, Maine 04096. Telephone: 207-846-3351. Innkeepers: Fred and Colleen Webster. 18 rooms in 4 houses, 11 cottages, all with private baths. 19 units with kitchens. 15 fireplaces. Rates from $21.00 to $95.00 from 1 to 6 people. Weekly housekeeping rates & European Plan. Open early June to mid-October. Leave Maine Turnpike at Exit 9 to Route 1, north. Turn right at Tuttle Road to Route 88. Turn left and follow signs to Homewood. This lovely old homestead has opened wide its arms with a scatter of cottages, so that more people can enjoy the many pleasures of Casco Bay. The Inn is only two miles from Yarmouth, a picturesque coastal village with churches, shops, and historical attractions. Borrow a bicycle built for two and bike along country roads. 🖝 Moor your boat at the inn moorings, and stay awhile till you get your land legs back.

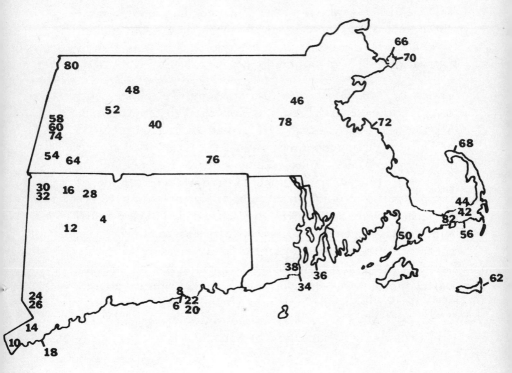

Connecticut
(Western)

(Eastern)

Rhode Island

Massachusetts
(Western)

(Central)

(Eastern)

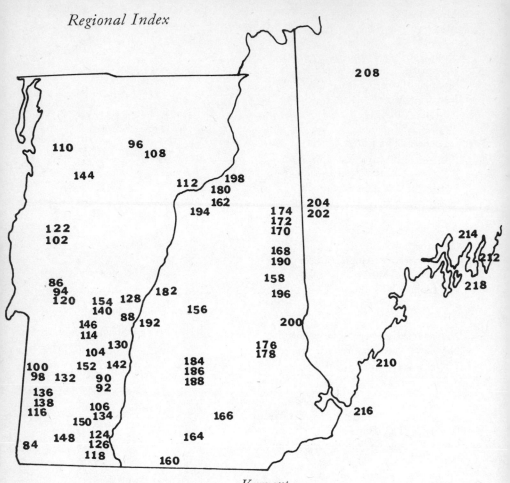

Vermont
(Northern)

(Southern)

Guests

Ye are welcome here,
be at your ease
Go to bed when you're ready
get up when you please.
Happy to share with you
such as we've got
The leak in the roof
the soup in the pot.
Ye don't have to thank us,
or laugh at our jokes
Sit deep and come often
you're one of the folks.

Found in an inn, Brookline, Mass.

When the stars are lost and rain seeps coldly upon the ground, how wonderful to find a lighted inn.

A well run inn and a man on a diet go together about as well as an arsonist and a bale of hay.

The cheers of millions are for politicians, while the quiet appreciation of a well cooked chop is but for a few.

A good country inn should have a dog.

I love all good inns, but secretly I have a rather special fondness if the boniface is fat.

The Pequot Press

Old Chester Road
Chester, Conn. 06412

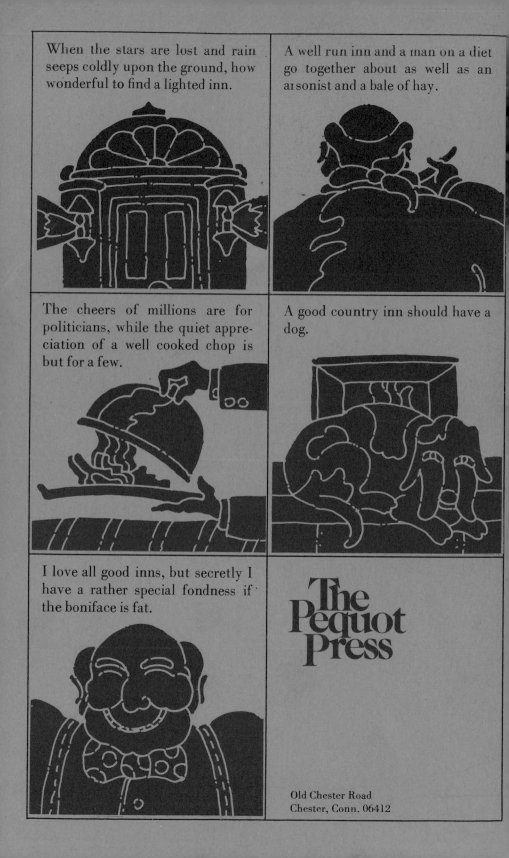